A Parrot's Fine Cuisine Cookbook and Nutritional Guide by Karmen Budai and Shean Pao

Published by Quietlight Productions, P.O. Box 58033 North Palm Springs, California, 92240

www.parrotsfinecuisine.com

Article contributors: Dr. Jason Crean, Dr. Stephanie Lamb, and Marlene Mc'Cohen

Cover, Layout, and Design by Quietlight Productions
Recipes and recipe photos by Karmen Budai
Editor: Roccie Hill

ISBN-13: 978-1-7323206-0-4

A Parrot's Fine Cuisine Cookbook & Nutritional Guide

By

Karmen Budai & Shean Pao

We would like to offer our heartfelt gratitude
to the following contributors

Dr. Jason Crean

Dr. Stephanie Lamb

Marlene Mc'Cohen

And a special thank you to all the wonderful bird owners
who strive to improve the quality of their parrots' lives

Buck, an amazing African Grey parrot, has a mom who needs a heart.
Please think about donating a small amount
to give his mom, Niecey, a chance at life.
www.gofundme.com/heartandmstreatment

Lastly - we would be so grateful if you would leave us a review.
Reviews are very important and help other parrot lovers find our book.
Thank you!

CONTENT

Introduction

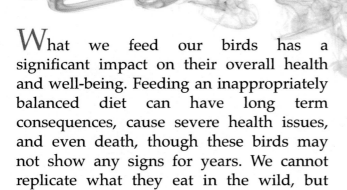

What we feed our birds has a significant impact on their overall health and well-being. Feeding an inappropriately balanced diet can have long term consequences, cause severe health issues, and even death, though these birds may not show any signs for years. We cannot replicate what they eat in the wild, but instead, we use this concept as a guide to create a well-balanced diet for them.

This book will guide you through the various topics on healthy diets for parrots, and will help you to make informed decisions when caring for such an amazing and fragile species.

POLLY'S STORY
By Karmen Budai

Sometimes, the smallest things take up the most room in your heart…

Karmen and Polly

That is exactly how it sums it all up for me. Once you become a parrot parent (or parront) there is no way back. They suck you right in with so much cuteness, fluffiness, and unconditional love that is hard to resist. I can now say that I am a very proud owner of the most gorgeous Lesser Sulphur Crested Cockatoo, called Polly. She's been part of our family for over a year now, and let me tell you, she has already stolen our hearts. Our entire household works around her. This little bundle of joy is full of life. She is a young spirit and will not let us rest for one second.

I was always more of a dog or cat person growing up, and never thought I could fall in love with a bird. I never imagined birds could be so affectionate or so sensitive. It wasn't until I was married that my husband introduced me to parrots. He had been around them since his childhood. And that's where it all began…

I started seeing them in zoos and was fascinated by their intelligence and appearance. It took us a long time to finally make that big decision as we had to consider all the important aspects of fitting this kind of commitment into our lives. We had done considerable research and were trying to decide which species would suit our family and lifestyle the best. It came down to either the African Grey or the Cockatoo. I was pro Cockatoo and my husband had always dreamed of an African Grey. Well guess who won ….?

We chose the Cockatoo for various reasons. First: they are love sponges and that's what our family is about – affection. Second: they are loud … well we can be, too, at times, so that fit right in. Third: they're smart, funny, curious, and mischievous. I could continue on and on, BUT the most important thing I wish to say is that they will become your lifetime commitment companion.

We love Polly to pieces, but it is hard work trying to give her the best quality of life. We know we'll never be able to offer her the same living conditions that she would have in the wild, yet she will never be hunted by predators, endure severe weather conditions, or, and here I have to laugh, go hungry. You will see why in a bit. These fragile creatures are not designed to live in our houses, but we have chosen to shelter them under our roofs, and so we have to do our best to make their lives enjoyable and provide a safe environment.

We went through some rough times with Polly when she became seriously ill. At the

the importance of a raw food diet. I learned how the correct diet can benefit the bird's well-being long-term. After what our Polly had been through, I decided to make that change and give my bird the opportunity to thrive.

I was also discovering how beneficial certain medicinal teas can be for our birds. I decided to see if they would help Polly. However, the company I wanted to purchase them from did not ship to the UK. That's how Shean Pao came into our life with her flock. I met Shean on a Facebook group called Parrot Station during the time Polly was sick. We were total strangers until my unfortunate circumstances with Polly connected us, and she kindly offered to ship me this special tea from the U.S. Since then, she has become my friend across the Atlantic, and we often share our new findings

time, we thought it was zinc poisoning but that ended up being a false diagnosis on the part of the lab. We couldn't understand why she kept getting sick on a monthly basis.

We were then referred to an avian specialist and Polly's blood was re-tested. This time there were no high zinc levels, but we were told we were facing a much more serious issue. She was diagnosed with a crop infection and was suspected to have PDD (Proventricular Dilatation Disease). There was also a concern she could have PBFD (Psittacine Beak and Feather Disease Virus).

It was the most difficult time and changed the whole mood at home. There were many times when we thought we were going to lose her, and that was something we could not allow. She spent weeks in the hospital over a period of four months, and eventually recovered after her long battle. She did not have either of those more serious diseases, which was a massive relief … never mind the vet bills.

During this time I began to look for some alternative holistic medicine. I joined Dr. Jason Crean's Facebook site and was fascinated by his work and knowledge on soaking and sprouting, as well as

on parrot health, diet and safety. The tea was a life-saver, and continues to help Polly maintain her health.

I began applying all of this new information I was learning, and started to create healthy salads and mashes, using sprouted and soaked seeds and nuts. I found I had a flair for turning the usual boring veggie bowl into something more exciting and visually more attractive. They certainly got Polly's attention. Creating this fine-dining experience for my bird became my passion. I started posting some of my creations on Parrot Station.

When I began to receive such pleasant and encouraging comments, it made me start thinking how I could turn it into a book that could help others feed their birds. Then I thought of Shean. I am thankful for her graphic design and publishing skills. She has put her heart and soul into *A Parrot's Fine Cuisine Cookbook and Nutritional Guide* and has helped me make it as beautiful as it can be. I'm very honored she has embarked on this exciting journey with me.

This book is where I knew I could share my knowledge and raise awareness on how important it is to feed your feathered friend a healthy nutritious diet. In this book you will find a variety of healthy recipes from chops to treats, all created using organic ingredients and all tested and proven by the fussiest beak.

Luckily this story has a happy ending and Polly has gone back to her normal health. Her new diet has helped her regain the weight she had lost during her illness, and she is happy and cheerful as ever. She is back to keeping us on our toes...

Karmen

3

Zen and Anaiah's Story
By Shean Pao

Zen

My passion for birds began in the third grade. My family moved to Oregon, and I was fortunate to spend a few magical years exploring a creek that cut between several miles of woodlands.

It was there that I discovered the beauty of birds. The Baltimore Oriole was my first love. A nest had been built along the creek in the hollow of a tree, and every day I watched the babies being fed. I became passionate about their life cycle. In my youthful zeal, I even decided to become an ornithologist. I often wish I had followed that dream.

Life changed course several times for me, but I never lost my passion for our feathered friends. Growing up, I owned parakeets, finches, doves, conures, and rescued many wild birds. I also spent time volunteering at a wild bird sanctuary that specializes in raptors.

I thought I had learned a lot about birds throughout my life, but then the internet happened. What a world changer. The internet connected all of us to information that had previously been difficult to find. And as time passed, our amazing collection of knowledge on birds expanded a hundred-fold.

It wasn't until I read Irene Pepperberg's *Alex and I*, as an adult, that my perception about parrots changed forever. Understanding the depth of intelligence in birds, and parrots in particular, reignited my fascination and love for these astonishing species. After reading everything I could for a year, we bought an African Grey baby. *Let me note here, that had I been aware of the desperate situation of abandoned parrots, I never would have purchased a baby. I would have found an adult bird that needed a home, which in fact happened six years later.*

CJ, our sun conure, and Zen, our African Grey, became our kids. I am sure there are many parrot parents out there who will sympathize when I express our obsession, and our love.

I would like to share two serious incidents that I experienced with my birds, and why my respect for our knowledge of avian health has grown, and how much we still need to learn about the care of our feathered babies.

Zen's story began when his wings were cut as a baby. I had planned to raise him as a flighted bird, having read about the importance of their brain development during their early years when learning to fly, but I forgot to remind the pet store of my decision. When I picked him up the deed was already done.

Zen is a big boy. When he flew and was forced down due to his clipped wings, he would land on our wood floors rather heavily. We didn't realize the danger he was in. Then we noticed there was blood on the cage bars, and we discovered that he had a wound between his tail and vent.

Because we live far from professional help, we received a lot of misinformation. Twice I made the mistake of taking him to people who said they had experience with birds, but who only made the situation worse. Please, if your bird is injured, take it to a certified avian veterinarian. Yes, you will pay a lot for it, but I would gladly have spent the extra money to avoid the extended suffering my Zen experienced.

I won't go into every detail, but in short, I took him to a regular vet. This person was supposed to have knowledge of birds but was not a certified avian vet. They gave us medication that caused Zen's scab to harden like cement and seep blood. Tragedy number one.

I sought help where I purchased Zen, again thinking this was a person who knew birds, and was told that Zen was plucking and mutilating this area of his body, though I had never seen him do so. We let them put a collar on Zen. Tragedy number two. After a couple of weeks, Zen was becoming depressed in his collar and he wasn't getting any better. I just knew I had to take him to someone I could trust.

Finally, I went to a well known avian vet, who was a two hour drive away. The first thing he did was remove Zen's collar. He explained that Zen was not plucking, but that his wings had been clipped too short. So every time Zen landed he had been hitting his rump on the floor, which eventually bruised and caused an open wound. In birds with different body shapes and weights, they often fall forward and split their keel instead. We had to keep Zen in a hospital box for many months while

he recovered. He was not allowed to fly, or to be more than a few inches off the floor since he might re-injure himself. It was a stressful summer for us all.

During my many visits with Zen's vet, he began educating me about parrot health and safety. Between his instruction and what I started to learn from Marlene Mc'Cohen's YouTube videos and on her Facebook group, Parrot Station, I realized I still had much to learn.

Today Zen is a beautiful, healthy African Grey, and I am thankful for the wonderful care he got from our avian vet.

Zen

Second Story: Anaiah
Six years later, we adopted a 12-year-old African Grey named Anaiah. We got her from a friend who was concerned because she had chewed off all of her red tail feathers and mangled the rest of her body feathers, as well. He wasn't sure what to do to help her.

I assumed Anaiah's problem was a bad diet. Anaiah had been fed a mix of colored pellets, seeds, and peanuts for her entire life. I was certain if we got her on a good diet with a variety of vegetables and healthy pellets that her inner stress would ease and she would stop plucking and recover.

What I've discovered since then is that our wonderful internet is very outdated. Nothing replaces a well informed avian vet. Fortunately, I made the decision to take Anaiah to an avian vet. A vet visit is something everyone who obtains a new bird should do.

Anaiah's vet started by educating me on feather plucking. He explained that 80-90% of the time that a bird starts to mutilate its feathers, it is because of internal issues. Plucking is a sign of stress. This stress can be caused by many sources: a poor diet such as sunflower seeds, bacterial disease, parasites, metal poisoning, allergies, exposure to cleaning products, or a host of other causes.

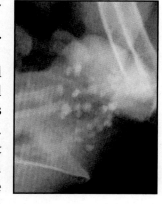

Anaiah was x-rayed. You can see the tiny spots in her gizzard where she had swallowed objects that were not food. The pieces turned out to be tiny rocks, and most rocks have some metal in them. It's where we obtain our iron, copper, and lead.

Parrots are so fragile. They can eat tinsel from your Christmas tree, or a single crystal from your shirt, glasses, or shoes. Crystals contain lead and will poison your bird. If the powder coating from their cage has worn off, chewing on the bars can expose them to zinc which will poison your bird.

Anaiah's bloodwork came back positive for lead posioning. Oral chelation dissolved the lead and surgery removed the stones. She came through splendidly, and I am happy to report that her red tail feathers are beginning to return.

Anaiah

During these events with Anaiah, I met Karmen Budai. She taught me about sprouting and soaking, and the amazing nutrients that are available to our birds through vegetables, fruits, and tea. I have learned that you can probably keep your bird alive on pellets alone, but what does that do to their emotional health and physical well-being over time? I can't imagine eating the same thing every day, and both Zen and Anaiah seem to love their meal times.

I know this has been a long story, but I hope I have helped make you more aware. If your bird starts to pluck their feathers, there is real cause for concern. Please take it to an experienced avian vet.

Thank you for your interest in this book. I hope these stories, articles, and recipes enrich both your understanding of nutrition and your parrot's life.

Blessings to you and your feathered kids.

Shean

Getting Your Birds to Eat Vegetables

By Marlene Mc'Cohen

One of the most common questions I am asked on my channel is, "How can I get my bird to eat vegetables?" I love this question. It means an increasing number of parrot owners understand the importance of providing nutritious food to their birds. But since no two birds are exactly alike, the approach may need to differ for each bird. However, my secret to getting them to eat vegetables is always the same: it's variety.

If you have more than one bird, you may find they enjoy completely different things. Half of my flock loves bananas, yet the other half will throw them at me just for offering them. You may have discovered that you have to play various tricks on your bird to get them to try the food at all. Although, it's not the "variety of tricks" that is my secret: it is the variety of food.

As a vegan, I believe it's important to feed my birds nutritious food. Although, while I maintain a healthy diet for myself, I am not skilled in the kitchen. I don't enjoy cooking and I haven't always been aware of other foods besides what I have already been eating. So, out of the hundreds of

vegetables that exist, you'd find me eating the same ten repeatedly. However, I am not alone, most families restock their kitchen with items they know they enjoy. So, in this case, my birds that love carrots, kale or Brussel sprouts were easy to feed, and I considered them to "like vegetables." Yet my other birds were difficult, picky, and were 'a lost cause.'

One day I decided to experiment and made a chopped recipe of new foods for my birds. The goal was to choose four leafy green vegetables, three red, yellow or orange vegetables, one or two fruits and a few herbs and spices. I set out with my 'bird safe' list, and since I wasn't making it for me, I gave myself permission to be creative. As you can imagine, I had so much fun choosing from all the mysterious leafy vegetables, that I'd never bought before like mustard greens.

My husband, George, helped me chop up all the vegetables and make a nice display as the birds watched curiously from their perches. My Umbrella Cockatoo, Jersey, wasted no time. She climbed down her perch, then up the bar stool and grabbed her favorite vegetable, cucumber. However, I wanted to introduce her to new things and not settle on her favorites while tossing everything else out, so I eliminated the cucumber from her mix just to experiment.

The first thing I noticed about our finished recipe was how colorful it was. Birds love color, so I was very optimistic.

Since our birds had been watching us make this chop for quite a while before we offered it, we didn't have to play any "hard to get" tricks as we might have if the food had come out of nowhere. They were already interested so that benefited the experiment.

My most curious birds are Picasso, my Mustache Parakeet, and Jersey. They are very trusting with food, so they will always at least try something I offer. Vinny, not so much. Vinny, my Galah Cockatoo, is suspicious by nature. The first thing Jersey and Picasso did was pick up different items and try them. They had to touch their tongues to everything before they committed to a favorite. They would consume that item, then move on to their second choice.

With Vinny, my approach had to be different. He isn't one to eat off my plate or with the other birds. I had to put the mix in his own bowl in his cage and observe him. Sometimes I had to hand the food to him directly, with repeated attempts, just to be certain he didn't want it. Vinny will move his face away like a child who refuses his vegetables. When I keep trying, he will take it from me just to fling it. But I find if I don't give up, he will eventually crunch into it. Once the juices flow out, he will realize he likes it. Of course, he will still drop it because that was his original plan and only when I try again will he take it. That is one of my many tricks.

Vinny ate several vegetables that day. It was glorious! As I watched my birds try these new foods, I learned a lot about the importance of variety. Since I had included things in the chop I don't usually give them, I realized that it's not that Vinny wasn't interested in vegetables, he just wasn't interested in the ones I had been offering to him. I also discovered Jersey liked bell peppers and Picasso enjoyed sweet potatoes. I was learning things about their tastes that I hadn't known before! To be honest, as a simple eater, I had never been motivated enough to buy watercress, yucca root or Swiss chard. It was exciting to find out that my birds liked them.

That's why a recipe book like this is essential for us to improve our parrots' health. It teaches us to explore new options for our birds, acts as an excellent resource for safe foods, but more important, it helps us introduce variety! For parronts that take pride in their cooking, exploring a new creation is always fun. But for people like me who are not experts in the kitchen, a book like this gives us an important guide to help our little companions who depend on us for their next meal. That means everything!

My "Variety of Tricks"

THE FUN TIME TRICK
One thing that works well for me is to give my birds a new vegetable during

"fun time." I do this when they are on their play stands and after we have had fun playing games and burning up their calories, making them hungry for a treat. This is a good time to introduce new foods to them since the bird and I have just built a lot of trust. I also want the bird to associate the healthy snack with fun. Even if we haven't been playing or dancing as my birds love to do, just the fact that the vegetables are in the bowl on the stand and not in their regular dish in the cage, makes it more exciting. In my experience, picky eaters are more willing to try vegetables this way. To accomplish this, their regular food should not be in the food-stand bowls. Their only option should be the vegetable or mix you are offering them. If the bird throws it, pick it up and return it to the bowl. They may give it a second look if they get hungrier. They always have their regular food in their cage to go back to so you don't have to worry about them starving.

THE TREAT BOWL

My birds always have two food dishes in their cage, one for their regular seed/pellet mix and one for their fruits and vegetables. This is useful to avoid cross contamination. Do not let the bowls mix and be sure to remove old food from their cages. But I also have a bonus bowl, "the treat bowl." This is a bowl that appears when I want to give them something special. The benefit of this is that after consistently putting their favorite treats in this treat bowl, they become excited to see what is next. When you add a new vegetable, they are more likely to associate it with a treat. This works particularly well with my Harlequin Macaw, Rocky. Rocky even asks for his own treat by saying "treat" in a cute voice. At that moment, he trusts almost anything I give him to be a treat and will give it a chance.

HARD TO GET

Playing "hard to get" with birds works amazingly well, not just with food but with anything you want them to be curious about. Birds have a flock mentality, so they desire to be included, but a lot of birds are also highly suspicious. Throughout my life, I have had many birds that favor the one person in the house who doesn't approach them with too much excitement or ignores them altogether. Some birds just do not appreciate eagerness and you can apply this to trying new foods... so here's what I do. I eat the food in front of him but don't let him have any. Try this and watch how he wants it more. Leave it within reach but when he goes to grab it, move it farther. This will increase your birds interest, and may heighten their desire to eat it.

THE MODEL / RIVAL TECHNIQUE

This technique, introduced by animal cognition scientist, Dr. Irene Pepperberg, is an effective way to train parrots. Use two people for this technique. One of you acts as the model and the other is the rival in front of the bird. The bird watches "the model" perform a task correctly and get rewarded. Then the two switch off. The parrot then learns the correct choice himself because he wants to beat the rival. I saw this work naturally between my birds Jersey and Picasso. The only time I have ever seen a bird try something it hated was when Jersey began eating carrots just because Picasso was always being praised for flying towards me to get one as a treat. I used carrots to flight train Picasso since he loves them. After he flies to me, I give him the carrot along with a lot of praise. This had been going on for years. Jersey had always tossed her carrots, but recently she has been snatching them from Picasso and eating them herself, which is truly amazing!

THE PRESENTATION

With birds, presentation can be everything, not just to make food look good but also making it shaped right. Sometimes birds can be picky about the way they hold things or even prefer certain vegetables over fruits because they don't want to get their feet wet. So pay attention to the things your bird enjoys. Are there things they have in common? What about the foods they throw? This can be revealed really well if your bird tosses something they would normally eat. You may learn a lot about your bird by investigating what the new difference is. Shape, size, consistency, time of day, not warm enough? Anything can concern these little obsessive beings.

THE MORNING MEAL

Birds are hungriest when they wake up. I find it easier to get my birds to try new things around the first big meal of the day. They also seem to be more willing to try new things when they are outside in their aviary.

MAKE MUSH

When all else fails, make your bird a mashed meal. Try sweet potatoes or oatmeal, and mix their chop into it. Warming it up can entice a bird to be more interested in eating, but never give your birds hot food. Birds love mushy foods because, as babies, they are fed through

regurgitation. During hormonal seasons, you may need to stay away from mushy foods and try one of the other techniques listed.

Even with all the tricks in the world, if your bird doesn't like bananas, he probably never will. Which is why variety is the most important factor! I know that Jersey hates bananas, but I will never stop offering it to her. You just never know if her mood will change like it did when she saw Picasso with the carrot. Quite often, birds don't give food enough of a chance. Even before they try it, they can be apprehensive. More often than not, you won't be able to get your bird to like a specific vegetable, but if you think outside the box and apply some of these recipes, you will be able to get him to enjoy "a vegetable" and that's all you can ask for.

The Importance of Raw, Whole Foods

Dr. Jason Crean

When I talk to bird owners, breeders, and zoo staff about nutrition, I often tell them that there is no "complete" diet for birds. What do I mean by this? Basically, we cannot expect to completely replicate the wild diets to which our species have adapted. Even in the wild, many of the foodstuffs that were once plentiful are on the decline. So what do we do? We should offer as much dietary diversity as we possibly can in an effort to satisfy all of the bird's individual needs. Food in its raw, whole form is the best, most efficient way overall to cover all of the bases. In my personal animal husbandry, as well as the recommendations I give the zoos for which I consult, I provide whole food diets in a variety of ways.

Birds, like most animals, require carbohydrates, fats and proteins. Some birds have more substantial requirements than others when it comes to certain nutrients but in general, we can be fairly confident in what we offer is safe and beneficial. Raw, whole foods may take many forms but the key is to offer unprocessed, unheated food in its whole form so that the nutrients are available to the cells that compose their bodies. Many oils fill the great need birds have for good, healthy fats. Carbohydrates found in fruit and vegetable matter are necessary for efficient energy expenditure. Proteins from foods like legumes and even edible insects can be a wonderful addition so that birds can get the protein they require.

I am often questioned about our birds' dietary needs and there are rarely easy answers. However, I do think it is safe to say that whatever food we offer must contain nutrients that are bioavailable. Bioavailablity involves the nutrient being in a form that the body can readily absorb and use. Raw foods take the form of fruits and vegetables, oils, seeds and nuts (both dry and soaked and/or sprouted), legumes, teas and flowers, and other healthy whole food items. Food items in their whole form not only possess important vitamins, but also the compounds that help the body actually absorb them. This is a problem with my vitamin supplements that contain the primary nutrient but not the associated compounds that help that vitamin to become assimilated into the tissues. This can also be seen with the different types of fats as some species better assimilate the fats found in plants over animals and vice versa. So let us start with fats since our birds require a great deal for optimal physiological functioning.

The F-Word: Fats are a good thing!

Essential Fatty Acids are often referred to as the "good" fats and avian requirements are substantial though all fats serve a vital purpose in the diet. EFAs are critical for normal reproduction, feather production and a healthy immune system. Animals require these fats to properly absorb vitamins like A, D, K, and E. These fats must be supplied by the diet but can be a bit difficult to offer because of their sensitivity to heating, processing, light and even agitation. When obtaining healthy oils for you and your birds, I always recommend purchasing them from the refrigerated oils section at a health food store or grocer. Plant oils high in Omega-3 (alpha-linolenic) fatty acids are needed for normal cell reproduction which is needed to replace old and dying cells and repair damaged cells. They also are needed to produce the hormones that regulate many physiological processes. They also help

regulate the production of eicosanoids, molecules that help maintain a normal immune response like that of inflammation. A deficiency in Omega-3's may cause stunted growth, issues with vision impairment and motor incoordination, and immune dysfunction as discussed above.

Omega-6 (linoleic) fatty acids are a bit more readily available in the diet as our birds can easily obtain a sufficient amount in seeds, soy, grains and some nuts. Though I do not recommend soy due to its high levels of phytoestrogens, these fatty acids are required for healthy skin and strong feathers, normal reproduction, and maintaining normal organ function. Deficiencies in these fats may lead to a failure to gain weight, degeneration of liver and kidneys, behavioral disturbances, inability of wounds to heal sufficiently, infertility, poor or abnormal feather development and dry, scaly skin. It's all

about balance when it comes to Omega-3's and Omega-6's. Omega-6 fatty acids increase the normal inflammation response of the immune system and Omega-3 fatty acids decrease inflammation. When this balance is not reached, the immune system is either underactive or overactive, and neither condition is desirable.

Omega-3's can be a bit more difficult to feed in the diet but ideal sources include Brazil nuts, pecans, walnuts, hazelnuts, pine nuts, and seeds like pumpkin seeds and flax seed. Flax seed is quite fibrous so I usually recommend flax seed oil as a more bioavailable alternative to feeding the actual seed. Other oils like borage and primrose oil can also be quite high in

Omega-3's and can be offered in the same way as any other oil. One of the best ways for parrots to get their Omega-3's is nuts. Tree nuts are a fun, healthy snack that are low in saturated fat and cholesterol free. They are an excellent source of protein, fiber, trace minerals and phytonutrients and contain 90% polyunsaturated healthy fat that helps maintain a consistent weight. Soaking nuts and seeds just overnight can also make them much more digestible and their nutrient load more available. Peanuts are not a tree nut but are a legume that I avoid; stick with tree nuts like those listed above for a powerhouse of nutrients.

There is an oil, however, that is one of the most versatile and beneficial sources of fats you can offer: coconut oil. My own avian veterinarian and international veterinary consultant, Karen Becker, DVM, NMD, has been a very vocal proponent of the use of coconut oil in not only birds, but also in reptiles, dogs, cats and small mammals. Coconut oil is the richest known source of medium chain triglycerides (MCTs) which the body uses as an efficient source of energy without the need for insulin production. It is highly digestible and, therefore, great for gastrointestinal issues and can be heated without risk. This oil is an excellent source of lauric acid which has antibacterial, antiviral, and antifungal properties.

Coconut oil has been known to reduce the risk of cancer and other degenerative conditions like arthritis. Even though it is a saturated fat, it supplies fewer calories than other fats and it actually improves cholesterol levels and helps fight heart disease. Many have used it, including myself, for weight loss as it helps balance the body's metabolism and hormones. Our birds can greatly benefit from this dietary addition as it aids the rejuvenation of the skin and feathers. It supports a healthy bone density, something particularly important for birds that already have hollow bones and can lose significant levels of calcium during egglaying. It also has been know to reduce allergic reactions, including those pesky seasonal allergies. Using coconut oil can be quite easy as it melts into a clear liquid just above room temperature. We have offered it in its whole form to birds who relish the taste and have mixed it with food where it provides a layering of nutrients on already healthy foods.

Energize with Carbohydrates

Carbohydrates are another nutrient source that can be vital for energy as they are broken down into simple sugars that the body's cells use as an energy source. Carbohydrates that are insoluble and typically indigestible are known as fiber as they are rich in cellulose. This helps prime the digestive system and can be obtained through many different plant sources. Grains like wheat and rice are a source of carbohydrates and legumes, fresh fruits and vegetables also provide all of these natural sugars from which birds can benefit. There are two main things I always keep in mind when I consider carbohydrates: processing and diversity. I use no processed sugars and the only carbohydrates that we offer birds in any setting are those that are consumed within their raw, whole form. Diversity in the diet also helps to keep the concentration of any one nutrient from becoming excessive. It is common knowledge that fresh foods are beneficial and this is where the benefits of carbohydrates come into play.

The Power of Proteins

Proteins are responsible for a great deal of the body's structural supports and chemical reactions that are involved in the organism's metabolism that allow the body to function optimally. Diversity is also key when it comes to proteins. Protein diversity and enrichment is critical to satisfying the amazingly varied nutritional requirements of our birds. Too much of any one thing is not recommended, no matter how healthy so the exact same combination of dietary items every single day is not recommended. By always keeping the bird's physiology guessing with various food sources helps to avoid complacency and dependency on individual food items.

Enzymes are proteins that start and maintain the ongoing chemical reactions through-out the body. There are two main types of enzymes: metabolic and digestive. Metabolic enzymes are found in the blood, organs and tissues and catalyze reactions that produce energy. They are critical for detoxification and the maintenance of normal body functions. Digestive enzymes are mainly secreted by the pancreas and are mandatory for the breakdown of food. They also assist in the assimilation of nutrients, increasing their absorption. Enzymes include examples like amylase that break down carbohydrates, lipase that is responsible for metabolizing fats, and protease that converts proteins into its building blocks, amino acids. We have all heard that birds should not have dairy in significant quantities; this is mainly because birds do not produce lactase, the enzyme responsible for breaking down the carbohydrate lactose found in milk. As birds never produce milk for their young, they never produce the lactase enzyme.

Raw, whole foods are generally rich with these all important enzymes. All raw foods contain enzymes but processing that includes heating destroys these enzymes as they typically denature above 110 degrees Fahrenheit. Sprouts are one of the richest sources of enzymes and some favorites that contain a high level of these enzymes are garbanzo, alfalfa, millet, sesame, sunflower, quinoa, and wheat. There is a great deal of information regarding the art of sprouting and that itself could be its own article but feeding seeds,  nuts and grains after soaking even just overnight can help to provide a powerhouse of enzymes in the diet.

What do I do now?
What you need is whole, raw food that is fresh and clean. My philosophy has always been that avian diets should be predominately unadulterated, unprocessed food that includes a great variety of items on any given day. What you don't need is anything with added salt, fat and sugar, fried foods, dairy products, or foods with additives and preservatives. Pesticides, herbicides, and fungicides should be avoided at all costs as the long-term effects are either unknown or have been known to wreak havoc on animal physiology. Things to add to your bird's diet should include organic foods including sprouts and other fresh foods, teas, nuts, and healthy oils. Any time a food is heated, it alters the nutrients and leads to an increase in carcinogens like advanced

glycation end products (AGEs) and acrylamide. These potentially harmful compounds are not tested for in commercially processed foods and are found in a great many of these processed foods.

Stress is a part of any organism's life and it helps the individual cope and respond appropriately to the constant stimuli that surround it. The more stressed a birds' environment, including inappropriate foods, exposure to chemicals in the home and water, lack of exercise, and emotional stress, the more they require certain vitamins and minerals to cope with these stressors. The best source of these vitamins and minerals is raw, whole foods. Nutritional variety is critical for good avian health and supplying correct nutrition prior to disease ensures the strongest vitality. Though this article is far from being a complete resource, its purpose is to spark some ideas as to how to reassess how we feed our birds. Our continuous focus should be on moving our birds from surviving to thriving, so keep offering whole, living foods and your birds will live wonderfully vibrant lives.

Reprinted with permission from In Your Flock companion parrot magazine, April/May 2014 is Vol. 2, No. 4

The Use of Tea in Avian Husbandry

BY DR. JASON CREAN

Though water quality is important for our avian companions, what birds drink in the wild is far from sterile. It is commonly known that many species of birds visit water sources like tree hollows in which plant components leach their tannins and other compounds and minerals. And many of us have seen wild birds drinking from "dirty" puddles and other water sources that are brewing with fallen leaves and mud.

The common tea leaf is from the plant *Camellia sinensis*, a flowering shrub native to China but that is only one of the many sources of the teas we brew and use. Flowers, leaves, twigs, herbs, and roots blended together with natural waters brewed by the sun's heat create natural teas in the environment. There are many health benefits to those who drink brewed teas to us and our birds. Tea blends can help birds in a variety of ways such as skin and feather quality, immune system function, detoxification and improving organ function, digestive aids, respiratory health, weight loss and fat oxidation, and hormonal issues.

The purpose of this article is to simply share our experiences with the use of teas in our program. Special thanks to avian veterinarian and integrative medicine specialist Karen Becker, DVM, NMD who has increased our knowledge on this topic and was the impetus for our research. We have incorporated these teas into our avicultural program and continue to recommend these additions to zoos and other institutions that have birds as part of their collections.

Different types of *Camellia* teas are commonly used and they differ according to the time the leaves are harvested and the process used to prepare them. They differ in their benefits to animal physiology. It is important to mention that *Camellia* teas contain caffeine so they should be decaffeinated by way of a process using carbon dioxide (CO_2) and / or water, but not chemically treated. Many commercial teas may say "naturally decaffeinated" but use ethyl acetate which should be avoided. It is essential to choose your teas wisely and buy organic loose leaf teas whenever possible.

Teas from the *Camellia* plant include the popular green and black teas, as well as white and oolong teas. Green tea consists of young leaves that are picked and dried quickly to avoid oxidation. Oxidation is simply the absorption of oxygen by the leaves when

drying which causes biochemical changes to the leaves, similar to fermentation. We've all seen oxidation at work when apples turn brown after being sliced. Black teas are completely oxidized before firing, giving them a more wilted look. White tea is picked before the leaf buds have even opened and they are steamed and quickly dried and are, therefore, also not oxidized. Each of these teas has its own benefits for you and your birds.

A note about caffeine: only teas from the *Camellia* plant contain caffeine. These include green, black, white and oolong. All other teas are considered herbal and are caffeine-free. When herbal teas are mixed with *Camellia* teas like green or black, you must be sure they have been properly decaffeinated. Using loose leaf organic teas

is the foolproof way to avoid chemically decaffeinated teas.

Herbal teas originate from plentiful sources of various flowers, leaves, buds, seeds, and other plant components. Each herbal tea has its own set of health benefits according to its chemical composition. The following is just a sample of tea blends that are used and their potential benefits for you and your birds:

Skin & Feather Quality

It is no secret that many of our birds are living in environments that vary in temperature and humidity much more than their natural, wild habitats. It also should not surprise any of us that some of our birds deal with emotional issues that manifest themselves in a variety of different ways. The condition of the skin and feathers is often our first clue that something may be wrong. For these reasons, we attempt to offer a blend of teas that are not only good for the body but also the mind.

Immune System Function

Green tea's properties have been well-established and are frequently in the news. Green tea possesses potent polyphenols, antioxidants found in plants that have amazing benefits that include regulating cholesterol, reducing blood pressure, and aiding weight loss. Professional research journals have cited additional benefits such as preventing gene damage which can lead to cancer, reducing heart disease and decreasing the incidence of stroke. Green tea also helps boost the immune system. Green tea is one of the teas that comes from the *Camellia* plant and, therefore, contains caffeine. It is vitally important to purchase organic, loose leaf green tea that has been decaffeinated by water or carbon dioxide. Rose and rose hips are also effective in increasing immune system function as they are high in vitamin C and bioflavonoids. Hibiscus shares some of the benefits of roses but also aids in moods and depression and helps to expel toxins from the body. Hibiscus, when steeped, results in a rich, red liquid that birds seem to find interesting so hibiscus is often used in blends to entice birds who may be suspicious.

Detoxification
Liver, Kidneys, and
Organ Function

Black tea possesses antioxidants that help maintain healthy blood vessels and promote healthy blood flow. We also use black tea specifically for our softbill breeders and pets, like our aracaris, which are prone to iron storage disease as the tannins present in the tea bind to dietary iron and prevent it from being stored in the liver. Many aviculturists use black tea for other iron-sensitive species like mynahs, starlings, and lorikeets and zoos around the world have seen its benefits for some time. Red rose petals, rose hips, and hibiscus are also potent blood, liver and kidney tonics, helping to cleanse the body and even help the body recover from fatigue. Dandelion leaf is packed with vitamins and minerals, including the all-important calcium, and aids digestion and liver function. Much like green tea, dandelion leaf also helps with weight loss in obese birds, an advantage for birds with fatty liver issues. Many veterinarians prescribe milk thistle with the knowledge that it aids the body in cleansing the liver and is used for the treatment of liver disease. It is also an important addition for the treatment of kidney and bladder problems. When brewing milk thistle, it is the seed that should be steeped in order to release the beneficial components from the tough seed casing.

Digestive Aids

Chamomile, as an anti-inflammatory, serves as a digestive aid by acting as a calming agent. Many people drink chamomile to calm stomach upset and we can extend these benefits to our companion animals. Peppermint is also effective in soothing digestive upset, a reason why mints are offered after meals in restaurants. Peppermint also can mask strange tastes and make your birds more apt to try new things. It has antiseptic properties and contains compounds that are believed to possess antiviral properties as well. Red, or rooibos, tea is a powerful anti-spasmodic which helps with easing the symptoms of digestive stress like colic and is also rich in minerals. It is known for calming muscle spasms and indigestion as well as possessing anti-allergenic and anti-inflammatory properties. Coriander is another component of this blend as it not only is used to treat digestive disorders but also is an appetite stimulant. Its pungent odor makes it attractive to many and, because the seeds themselves are brewed, contains important fatty acids like oleic and linolenic acids.

Respiratory Health

Anise seed, or "star anise," is effective in treating respiratory irritation like bronchitis. It can be used to halt coughing and soothe inflamed airways because of the presence of shikimic acid, which is also the primary ingredient in products like Tamiflu. With its pungent, licorice-like odor, the entire star-shaped seed pod is brewed to release these powerful components. Rooibos tea is also helpful due, in part, to its anti-spasmodic agents in calming the respiratory system. Red clover is also helpful in calming respiratory irritations, and lavender, due to its essential oils, is effective in relaxing the airways and calming the bird during respiratory stress.

Weight Loss and Fat Oxidation

Many of our birds, who are adapted for long periods of daily activity, tend to get a bit overweight in our homes. We can, however, help them to break down these stored fats, or oxidize them, so that the fats are more manageable by the body and used as an energy source. Some species are more prone to conditions like fatty liver disease and thus, may be in even greater need of these teas. First and foremost, green tea is highly effective in oxidizing stored fat. Green tea also increases the good (HDL) cholesterol and decreases the bad (LDL) cholesterol. Jasmine, sometimes referred to as "dragon pearls," is a flower that is brewed and helps in reducing fat and cholesterol absorption. Hibiscus is also effective in weight loss and helps to maximize optimal digestion, all while flushing the body.

Hormonal Issues

Raspberry leaf is a tea that all bird owners, especially those with chronic egglayers, should have in their home at all times. Raspberry leaf is an herb that is brewed that helps stimulate muscular contractions. It is for this reason that it helps women during childbirth and thus, helps birds to pass eggs. It also contains calcium which is another benefit for a bird that is laying, regardless of the situation. It also has been reported that it aids in fertility. Red clover is also helpful as it contains phytoestrogens that can help balance hormone levels. Coriander is also beneficial because of the many essential oils that are released from the seed when steeped.

Deodorizing

It is no secret that birds need to bathe. In the wild, they are bathing in the same aforementioned water sources that contain many plant components. We have found brewing teas can help cleanse birds while deodorizing feathers naturally. Flowers like yarrow, lavender, roses and chamomile when brewed and sprayed onto feathers help stimulate birds to consume these teas while preening. Since these flowers are so aromatic, especially lavender, just the smell can have a very calming effect on birds.

The following is just a sample of teas that are used and their potential supportive benefits:

Green tea's properties have been well-established and are frequently in the news. Green tea possesses potent polyphenols, antioxidants found in plants that have amazing benefits that include regulating cholesterol, reducing blood pressure, and aiding weight loss. Professional research journals have cited additional benefits such as preventing gene damage which can lead to cancer, reducing heart disease and decreasing the incidence of stroke. Green tea has been reported to boost the immune system.

Black tea also possesses antioxidants that appear to help maintain healthy blood vessels and promote healthy blood flow. We use black tea specifically for our softbill breeders and pets, like our green aracaris, which are prone to iron storage disease as the tannins present in the tea bind to dietary iron and prevent it from being stored in the liver. Many aviculturists use black tea for other iron-sensitive species and zoos around the world have seen its benefits for some time.

White tea has a host of important antioxidants that deter gene damage and inhibits the onset of cancer and angiogenesis. It also helps the body in breaking down cancer-causing agents and acts as an antibacterial, antifungal, and antiviral agent. There is also evidence that white tea supports bone health and density as well as enhances skin health.

Herbal teas

The following herbal teas originate from plentiful sources of various flowers, leaves, buds, and other plant components. Each herbal tea has its own set of health benefits according to its chemical composition.

Dandelion tea is packed with vitamins and minerals, including calcium, and aids digestion and liver function. It also helps with weight loss in obesebirds. It also possesses properties that can improve skin quality and thus, feather quality.

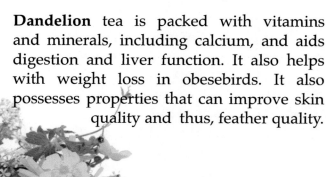

Chamomile tea is one of our favorite teas. The flower itself is used to brew this tea and, as many of us know, is very effective in settling digestive upset and calming the nerves. It also has antibiotic properties and relieves muscle spasms. We often use this with birds  that are prone to night frights as it acts as a natural sedative and helps eliminate insomnia, anxiety and stress. Thus, we have also seen it help birds that pluck or chew their feathers. Some pet owners who struggle with feather mutilation have even used chamomile topically in a spray bottle so that the bird ingests the tea while preening.

Milk Thistle tea also aids the body in cleansing the liver and is used often for the treatment of liver disease and has been used by countless veterinary practices for some time. It is also an important addition for the treatment of kidney and bladder problems.

Raspberry Leaf tea should always be available to breeders as it is a very useful and potent female tonic. It helps stimulate the muscular contractions in 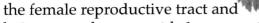 the female reproductive tract and helps pass the egg with less complication. We have used it successfully with egg bound hens and many zoological institutions use it with many different species, bird and others, that may have complications during labor or the passing of eggs.

Calendula tea is another favorite. It is actually a flower in the marigold family and contains fair amounts of beta-carotene. It has been used as an anti-inflammatory and anti-bacterial agent and is great for the skin. In our household, we use it ourselves for sunburn with unbelievable results. It also helps detoxify the body and helps limit the occurrence of digestive problems like ulcers.

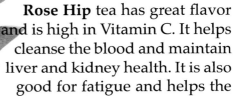

Rose Hip tea has great flavor and is high in Vitamin C. It helps cleanse the blood and maintain liver and kidney health. It is also good for fatigue and helps the body recover from illness.

Ginger Root tea has been used to relieve pain from arthritis and improve circulation. It helps eliminate nausea as well, one of the reasons we're given ginger ale when we're sick as youngsters!

Peppermint tea also has an irresistible flavor and is useful for digestive upset. This is one of the reasons peppermint candy is offered after meals in restaurants. It has antiseptic properties and contains compounds that have been reported to possess antiviral properties as well.

Rooibos tea is high in mineral content and has many advantages. It is known for calming muscle spasms and indigestion as well as possessing anti-allergenic and anti-inflammatory properties. It also works all the way down to the genetic level by maintaining chromosome integrity due to its anti-mutagenic elements.

Anise seed tea is effective in treating respiratory irritations like bronchitis. It can be used to halt coughing and soothe inflamed airways. It also helps quiet indigestion.

BLENDING IS KEY

We strongly believe in blending teas to glean the benefits and have individual ingredients support the others and the over-all health of the bird. For example, blending calendula and chamomile calms body and mind and is great for feather mutilators. There are other ways to glean the benefits of tea as well. When cooking for your bird, it is quite easy to substitute tea for water when preparing egg foods, beans, rice, pasta and other items that are prepared in hot water. Baking is another opportunity to incorporate tea by replacing water with tea in the recipe for bird bread, crumble, muffins or another concoction your birds

prefer. Offering certain teas without steeping them is another option, as small birds love to eat flowers, for example, within their dry food mix. For our softbills, we also roll items like chamomile or calendula flowers into our daily fresh fruit mixture for our birds to increase and diversify the nutritional content of every bite.

BREWING AND OFFERING TEA TO YOUR BIRDS

When first provided with tea, some birds will be suspicious so it is recommended to start out with weak tea and increase the concentration as they become familiar with it over time. You should always brew tea in hot, but not boiling, water to maximize steeping ability. It is also recommended to make use of a stainless steel mesh tea steeper when brewing tea and to always remove it before serving. It is not recommended to completely replace water

with tea, however, so as to avoid dehydration if the bird chooses not to readily accept the tea provided, especially in mixed aviaries where some species may integrate it faster than others. Since tea is a raw, whole food source, we offer it at the same time as other fresh foods and remove it when we pull those fresh foods to avoid spoilage. Fresh, clean water is then offered when tea is not. We recommend 1 teaspoon to 8-10 ounces of hot water to start and adjust the strength according to the birds' preference. Boiling water should never be used as it will destroy the beneficial compounds in almost any tea.

Some of these items can also be offered dry, especially the flowers. We mix dry flowers like Calendula and roses into dry seed mixes, especially for our smaller birds. There are other ways to glean the benefits of tea as well. Offering certain teas without steeping them is another option, as small birds love to eat flowers, for example,

within their dry food mix. For all of our birds, whether finch, softbill, hookbill, or ground bird, we also roll items like chamomile or calendula flowers into our daily fresh fruit mixture or mash to increase and diversify the nutritional content of every bite.

The use of tea is yet one more way to incorporate additional items to the diet and increase the amount of vitamins and minerals in your daily regimen. Teas can also serve as a great enrichment tool, using a different kind each day to keep things interesting. Mixing components of the avian diet in with dry teas increases foraging while also offering food items like flowers not always available in their fresh form. The many methods discussed here will hopefully allow you to provide more diversity in your birds' diets and help your birds to not just survive, but thrive.

Reprinted with permission from In Your Flock companion parrot magazine, September 2013 is Vol. 1, No. 7

SAFE FOOD LIST: **VEGETABLES** Curated by Dr. Stephanie Lamb

ENSURE THAT VEGETABLES ARE ALWAYS THOROUGHLY WASHED AND PREFERABLY ORGANIC

ARTICHOKE
BELL PEPPERS
BOK CHOY
BROCCOLI

BRUSSELS SPROUTS
CABBAGE: WHITE AND RED
CARROT
CAULIFLOWER

CELERY STALKS: SAFE BUT NOT RECOMMENDED. ITS LONG, STRINGY FIBER, IF NOT CHEWED, CAN CLOG A BIRD'S DIGESTIVE SYSTEM. CELERY LEAVES PREFERRED.

CHINESE CABBAGE
CORN: RAW OR STEAMED
CUCUMBER
CHILI PEPPER
ENDIVE
FENNEL
GREEN BEANS: RAW, NOT DRIED
HOT PEPPERS

ICEBERG LETTUCE: SAFE BUT FILLER FOOD. NOT RECOMMENDED SINCE IT OFFERS LITTLE, IF ANYTHING, FOR THE BIRD. OFFER ROMAINE OR BUTTER LETTUCES INSTEAD.

KALE
PAK CHOI (BOK CHOY)
PARSNIP
PEAS

POTATO: SAFE WHEN COOKED, BUT NOT RECOMMENDED. OFFER SWEET POTATO INSTEAD

PUMPKIN: INCLUDING SEEDS
RADISH
RADICCHIO
RED BEET: RAW

RED LEAF LETTUCES
ROCKET
ROMAINE LETTUCE
RUTABAGAS
SPINACH
SPROUTS
SQUASH: ALL TYPES. RAW OR STEAMED
SWEDE: RAW OR STEAMED

SWEET POTATO: RAW OR STEAMED, PREFERABLY LIGHTLY STEAMED. COOKING IT MAKES THE BIO-ACCESSIBILITY OF NUTRIENTS MORE USEABLE.

SWISS CHARD
TURNIPS
WATERCRESS
YAMS
YELLOW BEETS
YELLOW SQUASH
YUCCA ROOT
ZUCCHINI

SAFE FOOD LIST: **FRUITS** Curated by Dr. Stephanie Lamb

ENSURE THAT FRUITS ARE ALWAYS THOROUGHLY WASHED AND PREFERABLY ORGANIC

APPLE: REMOVE SEEDS

APRICOT: REMOVE PIT

BANANA

BLACKBERRY

BLUEBERRY

ELDERBERRY

BLACKCURRANT

BLOOD ORANGE

CANTALOUPE MELON: SEEDS ARE SAFE TO EAT AND NUTRITIOUS

CHERRY: REMOVE PIT

CRANBERRY

DRIED DATES

FIGS: RAW

GOOSEBERRIES

GRAPE

GUAVA

HAWTHORN BERRIES: REMOVE THE SEEDS AS THESE CONTAIN CYANIDE LIKE APPLE SEEDS

HONEYDEW MELON

KIWI: PEELED

LYCHEE (LITCHI)

MANDARIN: PEELED

MANGO: REMOVE PIT

MELON: SEEDS ARE SAFE TO EAT

NECTARINE: REMOVE PIT

ORANGE: PEELED - ACIDIC, FEED INFREQUENTLY

PAPAYA: SEEDS ARE SAFE TO EAT

PASSION FRUIT: FEED ONLY THE INSIDE SEEDS

PEACH: REMOVE PIT

PEAR: REMOVE SEEDS

POMELO

PINEAPPLE: PEELED - ACIDIC, FEED INFREQUENTLY

PLUM: REMOVE PIT

POMEGRANATE: REMOVE THE OUTSIDE SKIN

QUINCE

RASPBERRY

RED CURRANTS

STRAWBERRY

TANGERINE

YELLOW PLUM

SAFE FOOD LIST: **Flowers, Herbs, Nuts & Seeds**

ENSURE THAT FOOD ITEMS ARE ALWAYS THOROUGHLY WASHED AND PREFERABLY ORGANIC

SAFE FRESH FLOWERS

BOUGAINVILLEA
CALENDULA
CHRYSANTHEMUM
ECHINACEA
HIBISCUS

JASMINE: FALSE JASMINE (AKA YELLOW JASMINE/ CAROLINA JASMINE) IS DIFFERENT AND IS NOT SAFE

NASTURTIUM
PANSY
RED CLOVER
ROSEHIPS
ROSES

SAFE FRESH HERBS (AND SPICES)

ALFALFA
ANISE: LEAVES AND SEEDS
BARBERRY ROOT
BURDOCK ROOT
BASIL
BAY LEAVES
CELERY ROOT
CEYLON CINNAMON STICKS
CHAMOMILE
CHICORY
CLOVES
CORIANDER (CILANTRO)
DANDELION
DILL
GINGER ROOT
HORSERADISH ROOT
LAVENDER

LEMON GRASS
LEMONBALM
MARJORAM
MINT
NETTLE
OREGANO
PARSLEY
RASPBERRY LEAVES
RED CLOVER
ROSEMARY
SAGE
ST JOHN'S WORT
STAR ANISE SEEDS (POD)
THAI BASIL
THYME
TURMERIC ROOT

SAFE NUTS

ALMONDS
BRAZIL NUTS
CASHEWS
HAZELNUTS
MACADAMIA NUTS
PECAN NUTS
PINE NUTS
PISTACHIOS
WALNUTS: CRACK & CHECK FOR MOLD

SAFE SEEDS

ANISE SEEDS
CANTALOUPE SEEDS
CARDAMOM SEEDS WITH PODS
CARAWAY SEEDS
CHIA SEEDS
CORIANDER SEEDS
CUMIN SEEDS
DIFFERENT PEPPER SEEDS
FENNEL SEEDS
FLAX SEEDS
GRAPE SEEDS
MELON SEEDS
MILK THISTLE SEEDS
PAPAYA SEEDS
PASSION SEEDS
POMEGRANATE SEEDS
POPPY SEEDS
PUMPKIN SEEDS
SESAME SEEDS
SQUASH SEEDS

(Curated by Dr. Stephanie Lamb)

TOXIC FOOD LIST Curated by Dr. Stephanie Lamb

Toxic Bird Foods	Explanation
Alcohol	Alcohol should not, under any circumstances, be offered to a bird. It can be fatal even in small amounts. Access to it on a regular basis depresses their organ systems.
Apple seeds	Seeds of apples are unsafe for your birds. If chewed or crushed they release cyanide. If consumed in high amounts it can cause death. Contains amygdalin in high amounts in the seeds of fruits in the rose family which includes apples, almonds, apricots, peaches and cherries.
Apricot pits	If chewed it releases cyanide. Contains a plant compound known as amygdalin.
Asparagus	Asparagus has been reported to cause digestive upsets in birds.
Foods high in fat, sugar, salt	Avoid any "human snacks" such as chips, french fries, bread or other highly salted foods. High fat diets lead to obesity and can result in fatty liver disease. Avoid greasy, oily, or fast-food type foods, meat, butter, fried chicken, bones, sweets and any other processed food.
Avocado (entire plant and fruit)	Both skin and pit of this fruit has been reported to cause cardiac distress and eventual heart failure in pet birds. Unripe avocado contains "persin" which, when consumed in sufficient quantities, can cause illness or death.
Beans (any dried soup type)	Never offer dry soup type beans as they can be extremely harmful to your bird. Uncooked beans contain a toxin called phytohaemagglutinin or kidney bean lectin which is very toxic to birds. This is a sugar-based protein (glycoprotein) which is found in many types of beans. Soaking and cooking will remove the toxin, however will not provide any significant nutrition to your bird. Also avoid tin soup type beans.
Butter	A dairy product that birds can't process since they are lactose intolerant.
Caffeine	Caffeinated beverages such as coffee, soda, and certain type herbal teas can be extremely hazardous. Caffeine causes cardiac malfunction in birds and is associated with increased heartbeat, arrhythmia, hyper activity, and cardiac arrest. Stick to pure water and safe teas.
Carbonated beverages	Carbonated beverages contain carbon dioxide gas. It is likely to contain additives, sugars, high-fructose corn syrup, preservatives, caffeine, colorings, and should never be offered to birds.
Cherry pits	If chewed, releases cyanide. Contains a plant compound known as amygdalin.
Chocolate	Chocolate is not designed for bird's complex digestive system. Contains theobromine which speeds up the metabolism. Chocolate poisoning causes vomiting and diarrhea and affects a bird's central nervous system causing seizures and eventually death.
Dried fruit	Some commercially produced dried fruit can contain sulfides or sulphates and have nutritional loss due to the dehydrating process. Home dehydrated fruits are preferable and have some nutritional benefits, but they are still high in sugar.

TOXIC FOOD LIST Cont... Curated by Dr. Stephanie Lamb

Egg Plant	Fruit itself has not been recommended and was reported to cause some stomach upsets. Stem and leaves are part of the nightshade family and are toxic for birds.
Garlic	Garlic has similar chemical compounds as onions and contains allicin, which in rare cases can cause anemia.
Milk (Dairy Products)	Birds are highly lactose intolerant species and can't process any dairy foods as they have never evolved to produce lactase, the enzyme necessary to help digest lactose.
Mushrooms	Mushrooms are a type of fungus and have been reported to cause digestive upset. Caps and stems of some varieties can induce liver failure.
Nectarine Pits	Contain varying levels of a cyanide compound that can cause death.
Onions (Raw or cooked)	Can cause vomiting, diarrhea and digestive problems. Prolonged exposure can lead to a blood condition called hemolytic anemia, which is followed by respiratory distress and eventual death.
Olives	Contain high levels of sodium and are reported as toxic.
Peanuts	Peanuts are susceptible to contamination during growth and storage. This can lead to an infection by the mold fungus Aspergillus flavus, releasing toxic substance aflatoxins. Parrots are said to be up to 200 times more sensitive to aflatoxins than humans. It can cause breathing difficulties, decrease or loss of appetite, frequent drinking and urination, cyanosis (a bluish coloration of mucous membranes and/or skin), and even sudden death. Roasting peanuts reduces aflatoxin but does not eliminate it entirely. They have no nutritional value to birds and are high in fat. NEVER feed your bird peanuts! (monkey nuts)
Peach, Pear, Plum Pits	If chewed on, it releases cyanide. Contains a plant compound known as amygdalin.
Raw Honey	Should not be fed to birds due to high levels of botulism.
Rhubarb	Has very high levels of oxalic acid, especially in the leaves that are toxic to birds.
Tomato	The stems, vines, and leaves are highly toxic to birds. The tomato itself can be fed, however due to its acidity it is best to be avoided as it could potentially cause ulcers. This includes cherry tomatoes.
Tobacco (Cigaretes)	Smoking around your birds is never safe due to birds, very sensitive and intricate respiratory systems. Second-hand smoke contains over 4000 chemicals. Anyone breathing second-hand smoke is breathing in formaldehyde, ammonia, cyanide, arsenic, carbon monoxide, methane and thousands of other chemicals. Nicotine poisoning can occur if your parrot chews a cigarette. reported to cause panting, salivation, vomiting, increased heart rate, collapse, coma and cardiac arrest.

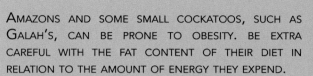

LORIES AND LORIKEETS EAT MOSTLY FRUITS, VEGETABLES, POLLEN, AND SPECIFIC COMMERICAL OR HOMEMADE NECTARS. SEEDS ARE NOT THE MAIN PART OF THEIR DIET IN THE WILD AND SHOULD BE OFFERED SPARINGLY.

MACAWS REQUIRE A DIET WITH A HIGHER FAT CONTENT. NUTS, SUCH AS BRAZIL NUTS OR WALNUTS SHOULD HELP.

AMAZONS AND SOME SMALL COCKATOOS, SUCH AS GALAH'S, CAN BE PRONE TO OBESITY. BE EXTRA CAREFUL WITH THE FAT CONTENT OF THEIR DIET IN RELATION TO THE AMOUNT OF ENERGY THEY EXPEND.

AUSTRALIAN GRASS PARAKEETS, COCKATIELS AND MANY COCKATOO SPECIES SPEND MOST OF THEIR DAY FORAGING ON THE GROUND FOR SEEDS. THESE BIRDS MAY BENEFIT FROM SEVERAL SMALLER FEEDS TO ENCOURAGE ACTIVITY THROUGHOUT THE DAY.

The Importance of Foraging

In the wild, parrots spend the majority of their day foraging for food. Their lifestyle in captivity encompasses a completely different experience. We provide them with daily "room service" that comes with nicely chopped up vegetables, fruits, nuts and pellets then serve it ready-made. If we have average work days, limited social interaction doesn't offer the bird much to do other than sleep or preen. Lack of activity and boredom can often result in frustration and behavioral changes such as aggression and reduced natural curiosity.

HOW TO AVOID IT?

Foraging is the best way to keep your bird busy throughout the day, keep their minds occupied, stimulate their curiosity and make eating more fun. Hiding food in various locations throughout the cage will keep them busy and excited.

Your bird will experience more physical exercise, help keep his nails and beak trim, and use his problem-solving skills like in the wild. Do your research on your own species as each has its own preferences.

Nowadays there are many wonderful foraging devices available for purchase or you can create them yourself, including fruit and veggie skewers, or foraging boxes. Some require different levels of manipulation or puzzle solving skills to uncover and remove the food such as turning wheels, opening lids, or unscrewing bolts. If you have never tried it before, start by randomly placing the items so they can be easily accessible, then work towards more complicated and challenging methods.

Happy Foraging!

Pellets - Pros and Cons

BY DR. STEPHANIE LAMB

Bringing a companion bird into the home requires commitment and dedication. It is our duty to see to it that they are cared for to the best of our abilities and one of the things that we can do to ensure this is to feed them an appropriate diet. Avian nutrition is a diverse topic as it varies across the approximately 10,000 species currently known to man. With members of the parrot family being one of the more commonly kept avian companions, our knowledge of their dietary needs has progressed throughout the years.

However, the issue of diet is a complex matter and not straightforward. Many variables will factor in to determine what a parrot needs in its diet. Species, age, sex, and health status all need to be considered. Our current research on parrot nutrition is scant and much is gleaned from what we know about other domestic birds like chickens, a few scientific studies on parrot species,

and anecdotal observations. In reality, it is unlikely that a complete spectrum of nutritional studies on all the species of companion birds will ever be complete. The reasons for this are many but include the vast amount of parrot species that would need to be studied, the prolonged time it would take to obtain the data given how long these animals live, and certain invasive procedures that would be needed to get complete nutritional information. Therefore, at this time we are forced to take the information we do know and apply it to the best of our abilities to formulate good diets for our feathered companions.

Currently, our most recent information indicates that parrots like to consume the reproductive parts of plants including fruits, seeds, and flowers. Furthermore, we can break parrots down in granivores (those that eat seeds), nectarivores (those that eat nectar), frugivores (those that eat fruit pulp), and folivores (those that eat leaves).

Additionally, there are some members of the parrot family that are considered omnivores because they will eat animal

proteins.[1] Most of the parrots that are kept as pets fall into the granivore category. However, even within this category there is variability. For example, although the wild budgerigar and the macaw are both members of the parrot family and are granivores, their dietary needs are slightly different. The budgerigar lives in an arid environment and is a ground forager who likes to consume seeds from low herbaceous plants like shrubs and grasses. Members of the macaw genus, on the other hand, live in a more humid environment and will forage out of trees for seeds, fruits and flowers.

The specific nutrients needed for a parrot also may change based on several variables. For example, when it comes to proteins, lorikeets are considered nectarivories and require only 3% protein in the diet if it is a high-quality protein.[2] Studies in cockatiels on the other hand show that 11% protein is required and in the wild because they will select seeds with a protein range of 8.8-14%. [3]

Additionally, life stage plays a role, as growing cockatiels have been shown to do best when given 20% protein in

the diet. [4] And this is just protein! Other nutrients like carbohydrates, fats and various vitamins and minerals will be different amongst the different species and their life stages.

Add to this complexity the differing needs of a parrot living in a home versus a parrot living in the wild. A parrot in the wild undoubtedly expends much more energy than a pet parrot in captivity as they must fly to various locations to search for their food and avoid predators. All the extra energy used in the wild creates the demand for a higher caloric need that our companion parrots could never approximate, even if they are allowed to fly around in our homes. Therefore, comparing the requirements of a pet parrot to its wild counterparts should be examined with caution.

When trying to prepare a diet plan for a parrot, much of the current information we have indicates that the addition of formulated pellets can be beneficial. Pellets provide a variety of nutrients as a compact, single unit. Pellets have their pros and cons, however, and these factors need to be considered when creating your own birds' diet.

The benefits to formulated pellets can be numerous. First, it is popular for owners to feed seed-based diets to birds; however, these types of diets are low in calcium, sodium, zinc, iron, lysine, methionine, and vitamin A. They are also high in fat and have an unbalanced calcium to phosphorus ratio. [2,5]

Formulated pellet diets are a better choice because the various ingredients that are added to make the diet will often supply these nutrients, along with many others, while providing a more balanced ratio.

Second, pellets reduce the ability for a bird to be selective and choose certain food items over others. Studies have shown that when a parrot is allowed to choose amongst various food items they tend to select higher fat items than is thought to be appropriate for their caloric needs.[5] It is generally thought that parrots require about 4-7% fat in their diet.[2] In a study with Amazons who were allowed to select from various food options (seeds, produce, and pellets) it was learned that they consumed seeds with the highest fat content and had about 20.6% of their diet as fat.[5]

Third, formulated pellets help busy owners, provide more appropriate nutrition than seed diets.

Pellets do have some issues that need to be addressed. First, parrots by nature are cautious and often fear new things. This applies to dietary additions as well. If a parrot has never seen a pellet before it will be less likely to try it right away. This can be perceived by owners as birds not liking the pellets and cause the owner to give up quickly.

Second, pellets are often uniform in appearance and shape and this seems to provide little stimulation for foraging behaviors.

Third, there is a growing concern for mass produced and genetically modified food (GMO) that is being engineered to withstand higher concentrations of pesticides. Certain pellet formulas may contain ingredients that have been processed in this way and these may not be the healthiest items for birds.

Lastly, and probably most important to keep in mind, we only have limited scientific information on the true dietary needs of parrots, and currently recommendations are based off of studies in commercial poultry, cockatiel, and budgerigars, as well as anecdotal evidence. Therefore, the current formulated pellets that are available are making the best assumptions as to what a balanced diet should be, but concrete information is still lacking and some of the assumptions we are making could prove to be false.

Pellets can be manufactured in various ways. Extruded, baked, and cold pressed pellets are currently available on the market.

Extruded diets are the most common processing method for dry pet foods and involve grinding raw materials, mixing them together, and then exposing them to steam, high heat, and pressure in an extruder machine. Certain nutrients can be lost though through this processing, including vitamin A, vitamin E, beta carotene, and certain B vitamins. [6]

Baked pellets also involve grinding up raw materials and mixing them together, but the product is then exposed to dry heat in an oven and vitamin loss is less. [6,7] A study in chickens showed baked diets had several more digestible amino acids than extruded diets. [7]

Cold pressed diets grind and mix ingredients together and then subject this mixture to being pressed to remove moisture. The product is then heated for a short period of time to give it the texture it needs. This type of processing maintains most of the original nutrients of the ingredients.

When trying to decide between the many different pellets that are on the market for your individual bird, it is important to take a few things into consideration. Reading the labels on the bag is a smart habit to get into. There are two key areas to pay attention to: the guaranteed analysis and the ingredients list. The guaranteed analysis allows one to see what the protein, fiber, fat and moisture levels are. Some will also include information about specific vitamins, minerals, or proteins.

Looking at this information helps one stick to certain nutritional parameters that are needed by their bird. If the information about a specific nutrient is not readily available, most food companies can provide

it upon request. The ingredients list is also important to evaluate to ensure that appropriate items are present.

Although research is limited on what items are detrimental to the health of parrots, there are certain things that may be best to avoid. From an anecdotal perspective, some birds have what appears to be a sensitivity to artificial colors. Sugar is often added to pellets, though not necessary. These simple carbohydrates are easily digested, absorbed, and used as an energy source, but with the relatively sedentary life style that our pet birds are afforded in captivity compared to their wild counterparts, they aren't needed. Additionally, the safety of certain additives like menadione sodium bisulfate, which is used as a source of vitamin K, has been questioned.

Whole, fresh foods are essential for holistic health. Various combinations of pellets and raw foods have been recommended and natural organic pellets fit more with the view of 60% raw foods: 40% pellets ratio. The key thing to keep in mind is that a variety of vegetables, fruits, grains, beans, nuts, and seeds are needed to create a well-rounded nutritional profile for the bird.

In short, it is smart to be conscious about what is in the formulated pellet you are using and whether it is a healthy choice for your bird.

References

1. Toft CA, Wright TF. (2015) The thriving parrot: The foods and beaks of parrots. In: Parrots of the wild: A natural history of the world's most captivating birds. Eds Toft CA, Wright TF. University of California Press, Oakland. pp 39-80

2. Koutsos E, Gelis S, Echols MS. (2016) Advancements in nutrition and nutritional therapy. In: Current therapy in avian medicine and surgery. Ed Speer BL. Elsevier, St. Louis. pp 142-176

3. Koutsos EA, Smith J, Woods LW, Klasing KC. (2001) Adult cockatiels metabolically adapt to high protein diets. J Nutr 131: 2014-2020

4. Harper J, Skinner ND. (1998) Clincal nutrition of small psittacines and passerines. Semi Exot Pet Med 7: 116-127

5. Brightsmith DJ. (2012) Nutritional levels of diets fed to captive Amazon parrots: Does mixing seed, produce and pellets provide a health diet? J Avian Med Surg 26:149-160

6. Cowell CS, Stout NP, Brinkman MF, Moser EA, Crane SW. (2000) Making commercial pet foods. In: Small Animal Clinical Nutrition, 4th ed. Eds Hand MS, Thatcher CD, Remillard RL, Roudebush P. Walsworth Publishing Company, Macerline. pp 127-146

7. Foreman AL, Fallon JA, Moritz JS. (2015) Cockatiel transition for a seed-based diet to a complete diet. J Avian Med Surg 29: 114-119

Parrot Safe Cookware

The simple act of cooking near your pet bird can potentially kill it. Still, many people are not aware of this danger and allow their birds in their kitchen area.

Obtaining appropriate bird-safe cookware is essential when you are considering having an exotic bird in your home. Birds' complex respiratory systems and high metabolic rate make them extremely sensitive to airborne toxins.

Teflon poisoning is the term used to describe polytetrafluoroethylene (PTFE) intoxication. PTFE is the non-stick coating used on many brands of cookware. PFOA stands for perfluorooctanoic acid, which is a petroleum-based product. It is a carcinogenic chemical used to bond the non-stick coating to the pan. When overheated, it breaks down and emits caustic (acid) fumes that are not harmful to humans, but extremely toxic to birds.

The safe choice to replace your Teflon pots and pans with is stainless steel, copper-clad stainless steel, copper, glass, cast iron, or ceramic cookware. There is some debate about ceramic brands that may also contain PTFE or PFOA. If you do choose a non-stick brand, make sure it is listed as PTFE and PFOA free.

COMMON SOURCES OF PTFE

It is not just your cookware that you have to be concerned with. There are many products that are potential hazards. Here is a small list. Non-stick irons and ironing board covers, pots, pans, cookie sheets, oven drip pans, broiler pans, pizza pans, slow cookers, griddles, woks, waffle makers, electric skillets, tortilla presses, hot air corn poppers, coffee makers, bread makers, space heaters, heat lamp covers, stain repellents, hair dryers.

Prevention

- Do not house your birds in the kitchen.
- Be aware that smoke from burned-on food, grease and other debris inside your oven can also be deadly to your birds.
- Do not rely on air filters or purifiers to remove toxic fumes from the air.
- Locate birds in an area where fumes and smoke will not drift into their airspace.
- Ensure that your kitchen is properly ventilated, preferably by a hood that vents outdoors.
- Never leave your cooking unattended.

Pure Water

Like all creatures that need water to survive, birds are no exception. Water makes up a large percentage of a bird's body weight and is critical for life. Although they can extract some moisture from their food, birds must have access to fresh, clean water at all times. Intake of water can vary per bird and will also vary per diet. If eating a mostly dry diet, then water intake will be higher than if eating wet foods such as vegetables.

The question is, which type of water is the best for them?

TAP WATER

In general, if tap water is fine for your consumption then it is safe, though not recommended, for your pet too. City water usually goes through a treatment facility and through regular tests where bacteria, excess minerals, etc., are filtered out. However, you can always have your tap water tested. If you have any doubt of its quality, have your avian vet evaluate it. There are also many home test kits available if you wish to analyze your drinking water. We prefer to use purified water to be sure our birds are not drinking additives which may be in your water, such as fluoride.

NATURAL SPRING WATER

Natural spring water is a type of bottled water that is a great choice for most birds. Always check the label to make sure the water is really natural spring water, though, and comes from real underground springs. This water will contain dissolved minerals. Spring water may be treated with ultraviolet light to kill organisms in the water, and may also be run through micron filtration, which removes particulate matter (such as fine sand, silica, etc.)

BOTTLED WATER

Bottled water is often just water from any source that has been usually treated by filtration. Minerals are then added afterwards (otherwise, it would end up being distilled water). The minerals that are usually added are magnesium sulfate, potassium chloride, and sodium chloride (salt!). Always read the labels.

FRUIT FLAVORED BOTTLED WATER

Waters containing fruit flavors, vitamins, or other chemicals to enhance the water taste is not safe for your bird and is not recommended for daily consumption.

CARBONATED WATER

This water has bubbles (either naturally occurring or added) and is not safe for birds.

DISTILLED WATER

Distilled water is a type of water that has been boiled into steam then condensed back into water. It has been stripped of any minerals and is considered tasteless. It is mainly used in steam irons and automotive cooling systems.

Drinking it can be dangerous, as demineralized water contains more hydrogen and is considered an acid (with a pH of less than 7). Distilled water will cause our bodies to pull minerals from bones to produce bicarbonate to neutralize the acid. This type of water should never be offered to your bird.

KEEPING WATER CLEAN

Protecting the water from airborne contamination or direct contaminants is important. This becomes a problem once water leaves the tap. Birds tend to dip food or defecate in their water dish. This material feeds bacteria and causes it to multiply in two to three hours. The most commonly reported waterborne bacteria is Pseudomonas. Other types of bacteria, such as E.coli, Klebsiella, Giardia, and Salmonella, can also grow in water. Any of these can cause diarrhea or other digestive tract disturbances, as well as more serious infections.

Provide your bird fresh, clean water in a bowl. Change the water at least twice a day, or more if the water has been soiled for any reason. If using a water bowl, cleaning it does not mean swishing it under running water. Thorough sanitizing in the dishwasher or with dish detergent then rinsing well in hot water is required for each wash. It is helpful to place the drinking bowls as far away from an overhead perch as possible.

Water bottles for most birds prevent contamination with food and droppings, however, there are many safety factors to consider, too. First, train your parrot to use it, then monitor that it is able to drink from the bottle.

Second, keep checking that there is no air bubble in the spout, making the bottle look full, but preventing your parrot from getting the water.

Third, cleaning the spout can be very difficult. If not cleaned properly, bacteria can grow inside the spout, potentially contaminating your bird's water.

Nutrition List

By Dr. Jason Crean and Karmen Budai

The nutrition facts list provided here is based on animal and human studies. Since very little research has been done on birds like parrots compared to that of mammals, we must use what we know and apply that knowledge to the physiology of other species. This coupled with what we know about the anatomy of parrots and their wild diets provides us with a foundation on which to build. It should be noted that the food items as listed are not meant to be medicinal in any way; information provided is what reports claim as far as how these nutrients support body systems. Additional research completed by the bird owner should be a continuous and sustained endeavour. As there is a great diversity of whole food items that are grown in a variety of environments, one should always consider soaking produce in a produce wash as well as scrubbing larger items (e.g. citrus fruits, pitted fruits, melons, etc) or vigorously agitating smaller or more fragile items (e.g. berries, leafy greens, grapes, etc). Offering a highly diverse diet of clean, whole foods is the best way to ensure companion birds receive the nutrients they need while enhancing their mental enrichment.

POTASSIUM

POTASSIUM IS A MINERAL AND AN ELECTROLYTE THAT IS REQUIRED TO MAINTAIN MUSCLE CONTRACTION, ASSISTS IN A RANGE OF BODY FUNCTIONS E.G. SUPPORTS DIGESTIVE AND KIDNEY HEALTH, REGULATES BLOOD PRESSURE, HELPS TO MAINTAIN A HEALTHY BALANCE OF FLUIDS IN THE BODY.

VITAMIN A

VITAMIN A IS A NUTRIENT ESSENTIAL TO A BIRDS' IMMUNE SYSTEM, KIDNEYS, SKIN, AND FEATHERS.

VITAMIN C

VITAMIN C A POWERFUL ANTIOXIDANT THAT IS ALSO KNOWN AS ASCORBIC ACID. PROTECTS CELLS BY SCAVENGING AND NEUTRALIZING FREE RADICALS.

CALCIUM

CALCIUM IS A MINERAL THAT SUPPORTS HEALTHY BONES, HOWEVER VITAMIN D IS REQUIRED TO AID THE ABSORPTION OF THE CALCIUM IN THE BODY.

PROTEINS

PROTEINS ARE ESSENTIAL MACRONUTRIENTS REQUIRED FOR ALL BODY FUNCTIONS. IT IS IMPORTANT FOR GROWTH AND REPAIR OF BODY CELLS.

BROMELAIN

BROMELAIN IS AN ENZYME THAT IS NATURALLY FOUND IN THE PINEAPPLE STEM AND FRUIT. IT BREAKS DOWN PROTEINS IN THE BODY AND ACTS AS AN ANTI-INFLAMMATORY AND ANTI-SWELLING AGENT.

OXALATES

OXALATES ARE A NATURALLY OCCURRING COMPOUND IN FOODS LIKE SPINACH AND CHARD. OXALATES ARE ANTINUTRIENTS THAT CAN PREVENT THE PROPER DIGESTION AND ABSORPTION OF SOME NUTRIENTS. THEY BIND TO MINERALS LIKE CALCIUM AND PREVENT YOUR BODY FROM ABSORBING THEM.

HIGH LEVELS OF VITAMINS AND MINERALS IN VEGETABLES, FRUITS, HERBS ARE MARKED IN BOLD IN THE NUTRITION LIST.

No Single vegetable should be fed exclusively. Variety is the key.				
VEGETABLES	NUTRIENTS	REPORTED BENEFITS	FREEZES WELL	COMMENTS
ARTICHOKE	vitamins **B12, K**, C, B6, magnesium, manganese, potassium, phosphorus, iron	detoxifies liver and digestive system, is excellent source of fiber, keeps blood sugar levels stable, good source of iron, prevents anemia	No	Great for foraging.
BEET	vitamin C, **folate, manganese, potassium,** calcium, copper magnesium, iron	cleansing, detoxifies liver and gall bladder, detoxifies the blood, contains anti-inflammatory properties	Yes	Great source of fiber to contribute to a healthy microbiome.
BELL PEPPER	vitamins **B6, C, A,** folate, potassium, beta-carotenes	vitamin A is a nutrient essential to a bird's immune system, kidneys, skin and feathers	No	The different coloured peppers available can help diversify the diet and enhance enrichment. Seeds may also be fed. Organic preferred.
BROCCOLI	vitamin **K, A, C,** B3, B5, **B6, folic acid, potassium, phosphorus,** high in protein, **manganese,** calcium, iron **magnesium**	antioxidant, intestinal cleanser, antiviral, antibiotic, stimulates liver function, lower blood pressure	Yes	Helps maintain healthy microbiota due to fiber content. Source of phytochemicals that is reported to support immune system.
BOK CHOY (PAK CHOI)	vitamin **A, C, K,** B6, **folate,** iron, **calcium,** phosphorus, magnesium, omega-3,manganese beta-carotene	antioxidant, one of the top anti-inflammatory foods, lowers blood pressure, lower in oxalates	No	Available year-round. Great for those birds with calcium deficiency.
BRUSSELS SPROUTS	vitamin **K, C, A, folate,** manganese, potassium, thiamine vitamin B1, iron, **omega-3 fatty acids**	bone building vitamin K, boosts immune system with vitamin C, improves brain health, balances blood sugar, restore digestive health, lower in oxalates	Yes	Enriching when fed on stalk to a wide variety of hookbills.
BUTTERNUT SQUASH	vitamin **A, C,** E, B6, **potassium, magnesium,** manganese, calcium	high in antioxidants, boosts immune system, reduces inflammation, keeps bones healthy, improves physical performance and reduces fatigue	Yes	May be fed raw or lightly steamed.
CARROT	vitamin **A, K, C, potassium,** calcium, magnesium, beta – carotene	cleanses liver, high source of antioxidants, encourages detoxing	Yes	Preferred organic. Vitamin A is a nutrient essential to birds' immune system, kidneys, skin, and feathers.

NO SINGLE VEGETABLE SHOULD BE FED EXCLUSIVELY. VARIETY IS THE KEY.				
VEGETABLES	**NUTRIENTS**	**REPORTED BENEFITS**	**FREEZES WELL**	**COMMENTS**
CAULIFLOWER	vitamin **C, K**, B6 calcium, manganese magnesium, **folic acid**, potassium, boron, beta-carotene	rich in antioxidants and anti-inflammatory compounds, supports liver and kidney disorder, reduces high blood pressure, helps balance hormones	Yes	Contains glucosinolates which are reported to regulate inflammation, immune functions, and more.
COURGETTE (ZUCCHINI)	high in potassium, **manganese, riboflavin,** antioxidants like vitamin **C**, A, **B6**	improves digestion, anti-inflammatory properties, boosts immune system, helps improve liver function and detoxification, high source of antioxidants and vitamin C, good source of energizing B vitamins	Yes	Low in calories and high in anti-inflammatory properties.
CUCUMBER	vitamin A, B, C, D, **K**, folate, manganese, calcium, magnesium, potassium	blood pressure,prevents dehydration, gout, hydrates and soothes skin, detoxify the body, helps alkalize blood, natural electrolyte booster	No	High in fiber and water, both of which are critical for healthy digestion.
CHILI PEPPER	vitamin **C, A, B6**	aids digestion	Yes	Contains capsaicin which is reported to have significant metabolic benefits.
DANDELION LEAVES	vitamin **A, C**, B6, calcium, iron, potassium, folate, magnesium, phosphorus, copper, high in fiber	settle digestion, strengthen bones, antioxidant lowers blood sugar, highly nutritious	No	Feed raw or dried.
FENNEL	high in vitamin **C, dietary fiber, potassium**, vitamin A, B6, K, folate, iron, calcium, magnesium, copper, zinc, selenium	help maintain bone health and strength, lowers blood pressure, aids digestion, improves skin health	Bulb yes, leaves no	Due to the high potassium content, those with kidney disease should limit the amount of fennel they eat.
GREEN BEANS	vitamin **C, K, A, manganese**, contains high levels of several proteins, carotenoids, folate	supports a healthy digestive system, keeps bones strong, helps maintain healthy eating habits	Yes	Legumes can be enriching as hookbills like to open them.
KALE	calcium, magnesium, phosphorus, potassium, vitamin **A, C**, E, **K** B6, folic acid, iodine, manganese	supports metabolism and digestion, detoxes stomach, stimulates immune system, kills bacteria and viruses, is potent antioxidant, promotes pro-inflammatory omega-6 and anti-inflammatory omega 3-balance	Yes	Good alternative to higher oxalate foods like collard greens.

Vegetables	Nutrients	Reported Benefits	Freezes Well	Comments
No Single vegetable should be fed exclusively. Variety is the key.				
Lettuce & Other Leafy Greens	vitamin K	lettuces like green leaf contain higher levels of vitamin K and romaine lettuce higher levels of vitamin A. Iceberg should be avoided when other types of lettuces are available	No	Most lettuces can be offered regularly aside from iceberg which has more water content.
Okra	vitamin A, **C**, B6 potassium, **magnesium**, calcium, iron, high-fiber food, pectin	provides ample calcium and magnesium, helping prevent both calcium and magnesium deficiency, naturally reduces cholesterol, good source of protein, helps stabilize blood sugar, good for digestion	Yes	Enriching for hookbills to extract inner seeds.
Peas	plenty of protein, vitamins **C, A,** B6, manganese, iron, dietary fiber, potassium, lutein, low fat	strong immune system, high levels of anti-oxidants, has anti-inflammatory properties, blood sugar regulation, improves bowel health	Yes	Best if soaked and sprouted.
Pumpkin (and seeds)	vitamin **A, C, E,** rich in dietary fiber, potassium, iron	rich in vital antioxidants, low in calories, seeds are an excellent source of health promoting amino acid tryptophan	Yes	Serve raw or lightly steamed. Seeds source of beneficial oil.
Radish (raw)	vitamin C, B6, potassium, folate, manganese, iron, potassium	alkaline-forming food that is very helpful in keeping pH balance in check, detoxification, skin health, zinc, phosphorus	Yes	Adds color and texture to batches of mash.
Rocket (Arugula)	vitamin **K, A, C, manganese,** calcium, folate	improves heart health, helps maintain strong bones, improves digestion, supplies important vitamins and minerals	No	Great green to mix with a variety of foods and mashes.
Romaine Lettuce	vitamin **A, K, C, folate, manganese**	excellent source of antioxidants vitamin A & C, boosts immunity, helps digestion & intestine health	No	Great alternative to higher oxalate greens.
Spinach	high in fiber, **iron,** calcium, magnesium, **folic acid,** vitamin **A, C,** E, **K,** B6, potassium	helps regulate blood pressure, boosts immunity, supports bone health, helps with detoxification	No	Feed in moderation as it's high in oxalates.

No Single Vegetable Should Be Fed Exclusively. Variety Is The Key.				
Vegetables	**Nutrients**	**Reported Benefits**	**Freezes Well**	**Comments**
Sweet Potato	excellent source of vitamins **A** (in the form of beta-carotene), B1, B2, **B6, C**, iron, **manganese**, copper, pantothenic acid, fiber, potassium	vitamin A – a nutrient essential to birds' immune system, kidneys, skin, and feathers. High in antioxidants, boosts brain function, enhances immunity	No	Feed raw or lightly steamed. Nutrients are more bioavailable if lightly steamed.
Swiss chard	high in vitamin **K, A, C, E, B2, iron, magnesium, potassium**, calcium, copper, manganese	high in antioxidants, maintains bone health, improves digestion, helps maintain healthy brain function, benefits nerve and muscle function	No	Colors can be enticing to picky eaters.
Turnip Greens	vitamin **K, A, C, E**, B6, **folate, calcium**, copper, manganese	high source of antioxidants, helps maintain strong bones with vitamin K	Yes	Source of dietary fiber that supports healthy gut flora.
Watercress	vitamin **A, C, K**, calcium, magnesium, phosphorus, iron, beta carotene, iodine, ascorbic acid, folic acid, iodine, manganese	purifies blood, provides beneficial anti-inflammatory effects, helps increase metabolism, contains useful omega 3s, lowers blood pressure	Yes	A nutrient dense food that can be easily mixed with other vegetable material.
Winter Squash (Acorn, Hubbard, Butternut etc.)	good source of vitamen A, manganese, potassium, beta carotene	vitamin A – a nutrient essential to birds' immune system, kidneys, skin, and feathers	No	Serve raw or lightly steamed. Seeds also good source of fatty acids.
Yellow Corn	high in **beta-carotene** and **lutein**, vitamin **B6**, iron, magnesium, **potassium**, folic acid, **phosphorus**	good source of antioxidants, high in fiber, slowly digested source of carbohydrates, naturally gluten-free	Yes	Avoid feeding corn when it's genetically modified, or found in other forms of processed foods.
Yams	vitamin **C, A, potassium**, manganese, **pyridoxine, copper**	strong bones, support healthy immune function, good source of energy	No	Never feed uncooked since they carry naturally occurring plant toxins including dioscorine, diosgenin, and triterpenes.

		NO SINGLE FRUIT SHOULD BE FED EXCLUSIVELY. VARIETY IS THE KEY.		
FRUITS	**NUTRIENTS**	**REPORTED BENEFITS**	**FREEZES WELL**	**COMMENTS**
ACAI BERRY	**manganese**, vitamin A, B1, B2 and B3, copper, iron, thimaine, calcium, magnesium, omega-3, 6 and 9	stimulates healthy digestion, helps with cognitive functioning	Yes	Rich in fatty acids, dietary fiber and antioxidants.
GRAPEFRUIT	vitamin **A**, **C**, B6, calcium, magnesium, potassium, folate	blood cleansing, supports heart health, prevent calcium deposits, helps boost metabolism, immunity booster, rich in beta-carotene	No	High in fiber, low in calories and moisture-rich, all of which supports a healthy digestive system.
APPLE	potassium, beta – carotene, vitamins A, B, B2, B6, **C**, **K**, pectin, calcium, chlorine, iodine, iron, magnesium, phosphorus, manganese	removes toxins, cleansing, lower cholesterol, aids digestion	No	If not organically grown, substitute pears, cantaloupe, kiwi, watermelon, nectarines, honeydew or bananas.
APRICOT	vitamin **A**, **C**, E, **K**, **potassium**, niacin, manganese, copper	high in antioxidants, reduces inflammation, protects the liver	Yes	If not organically grown, substitute nectarines, cantaloupes, and watermelon.
BANANA	vitamin A, **C**, **B6** pectin, iron, B-complex, riboflavin, niacin, folic acid, protein, **manganese**, **potassium**, magnesium, calcium, fiber	improve kidney health, aids digestion, boosting energy, loaded with potassium	Yes (peeled only)	Fresh, not overly ripe. Mixing with other fruit may spoil other fruit quicker.
BLACKBERRY	vitamin E (alpha tocopherol), **folate**, magnesium, **copper**, potassium, good source of dietary fiber, vitamin **C**, **K**, **manganese**	reduce inflammation, fight infection and boost immunity, promotes healthy skin	Yes	Preferred organic.
BLACK CURRANT	vitamin **C**, E, A, **manganese, iron, potassium,** magnesium, phosphorus, calcium	rich in anthocyanins, boosts immunity, protects again pathogens	Yes	Rich in anthocyanins which are powerful antioxidants.

		No Single fruit should be fed exclusively. Variety is the key.		
Fruits	**Nutrients**	**Reported Benefits**	**Freezes Well**	**Comments**
Blueberry	dietary fiber, **manganese**, vitamin **K**, E, **C**, B6, thiamine, riboflavin, copper	high in antioxidants, boost brain health,alleviate inflammation, support digestion	Yes	Preferred organic.
Boysenberry	vitamin **C**, iron, magnesium	maintains healthy blood pressure, improves digestive health, increases bone strength, healthy brain	Yes	High vitamin C content; use sparingly for iron sensitive species.
Cantaloupe Melon	vitamin **A, C**, K, B6, **potassium**, folate, niacin, magnesium, thiamine	great source of antioxidants vitamin A, C, contains anti-inflammatory properties, boosts immunity, good for digestion, helps the body detox, restores pH Levels	No	Offer flesh and seeds for enrichment.
Carambola (star fruit)	vitamin C, zinc, magnesium, fiber, phosphorus, iron, calcium, magnesium, sodium, potassium	anti-inflammatory, boosts immunity, balances blood pressure, improves digestion, improves respiratory health, improves metabolism, detoxifies the body	No	Despite having many potential health benefits, in individuals with kidney failure, this fruit should be avoided due to high levels of oxalic acid.
Casaba Melon	vitamin **C**, iron, calcium	maintains good general health	No	Feed flesh and seeds. Moisture-rich.
Canary Melon	vitamin **C, A**	support immune system, protects against free radicals	No	Feed flesh and seeds. Moisture-rich.
Cherry	vitamin C, K, A, B6, **potassium**, manganese, copper, magnesium	high source of antioxidants, reduce inflammation	Yes	Preferred organic; substitute blueberries, raspberries, watermelon and kiwis.
Cranberry	vitamin C, E, K, B6, **manganese**, copper, pantothenic acid, potassium	decreases inflammation, improves immune function, benefits the digestive tract	Yes	High in antioxidants, great addition to mashes.
Crenshaw Melon	vitamin **A, C**, iron, calcium		No	Preferred organic, or substitute other melons. Feed flesh and seeds.
Coconut Raw Meat	magnesium, zinc, **potassium**, folic acid, vitamin C, **manganese, copper**, lauric acid which has antibacterial & antiviral activities, contains large amount, medium chain fatty acids	rehydrating, reported that fat in coconut may possibly help to lower bad cholesterol levels and increase good cholesterol levels	No	Great source of fiber and fatty acids.

FRUITS	NUTRIENTS	REPORTED BENEFITS	FREEZES WELL	COMMENTS
\multicolumn{5}{c}{No Single fruit should be fed exclusively. Variety is the key.}				
DATE	calcium, iron, Vitamin B3, Beta-carotene	Relieves diarrhoea, supports respiratory system	No	Great source of dietary fiber.
DRIED DATE	vitamin A, C, E, K, B2, B6, niacin and thiamine	excellent anti-oxidant, improves muscle strength, great energy booster, packed with calories	No	See Date.
DRAGON FRUIT OR PITAYA	vitamin **C, iron**, rich in phytoalbumins which is high in antioxidants, good source of calcium and phosphorus	immune booster, digestion helper	No	Must be peeled; rich in phytoalbumins which are prized for their antioxidant properties. Also good source of calcium and phosphorus.
FIG - RAW	calcium, **potassium, manganese**, vitamin C, A, K, B6, beta-carotene, magnesium	mild laxative, clears toxins, high source of calcium	No	Very seasonal; great austerity fruit.
FIG - DRIED	**manganese**, zinc, vitamin **K**, B6, **potassium, calcium, magnesium, copper, iron**, phosphorus, thiamine, riboflavin	powerful antioxidant, antibacterial and antifungal, great source of potassium, fiber and other depleted nutrients	No	When dried, the health benefits of figs increase and so do calories.
GOOSEBERRIES	vitamin C, A, B6, manganese, potassium, copper	contains phytochemicals, promotes liver health, reduces cholesterol levels, controls blood sugar, prevents constipation, decreases inflammation, supports cognitive function	Yes	Source of dietary fiber to support cardiovascular and digestive health.
GRAPE	vitamin **K,** C, B6, copper, potassium, thiamine, riboflavin, manganese	loaded with antioxidants, anti-inflammatory action, antimicrobial benefits	Yes	Preferred organic.
GUAVA	vitamin **C, A, fiber, lycopene, folate, copper,** potassium, magnesium, phosphorus	boosts the immune system, great source of potassium for lowering blood pressure, stops free radicals	No	Has more powerful antioxidants than almost any other fruit.
HONEYDEW MELON	vitamin C, B-6, **potassium,** thiamin	hydrates the body, boosts immune system	No	Great fruit for daily use; moisture-rich. Feed flesh and seeds.

FRUITS	NUTRIENTS	REPORTED BENEFITS	FREEZES WELL	COMMENTS
		No Single fruit should be fed exclusively. Variety is the key.		
KAKI/ PERSIMMON	vitamin **A, C**, B6, E, K, **manganese**, copper, potassium, calcium, zinc	high in antioxidants, promotes regularity, supports healthy vision, reduces cholesterol levels, decreased inflammation, lowers blood pressure	No	There are astringent and non-astringent persimmons. Hachiya persimmons are common, astringent & recommended. Do not feed the peel. Very high in tannins if fed before soft.
KIWI	vitamin **C, K**, E, potassium, copper, folate	incredible source of antioxidant-powered vitamin C and E, improves respiratory health, aids in digestion, antifungal and antibacterial capabilities	Yes	Preferred organic. Do not feed fuzzy skin. Values change if fruit was held in storage. Feed in limited quantities.
LYCHEES (LITCHIS)	vitamin **C**, B6, magnesium, potassium, copper, phosphorus	aids digestion, boosts immunity, disease-fighting flavonoids, antioxidant protection, blood regulation, anti-inflammatory benefits, anti-viral activity	No	Use sparingly; very high vitamin C for iron sensitive birds.
MANDARIN (TANGERINES)	vitamin **A, C, B6**, calcium, potassium	anti-microbial properties	No	Skin also has reported health benefits; preferred organic.
MANGO	vitamin C, beta-carotene, potassium, calcium, magnesium	reduces acidity, supports kidneys, relieves poor digestion, good blood cleanser	Yes	Moderately rich in vitamin C.
MANGOSTEEN	vitamin **C**, A, iron, calcium	combats inflammation and allergies, lowers blood sugar, boosts heart health, bolsters immunity, aids digestion	No	Do not feed the rind, only the white inner fruit.
MULBERRY	vitamin **C, K**, E, iron, potassium, calcium, riboflavin, magnesium, phosphorus	decreases cholesterol levels, protects liver health, stabilizes blood sugar levels	Yes	Skin contains resveratrol which is a phytoalexin a type of plant antibiotic.
ORANGE	vitamin **C**, A, B6, magnesium, calcium, potassium	more powerful pain reducer and anti-inflammatory, proven oral health protector thanks to its antimicrobial capabilities, aids in digestion	No	Highly acidic. Feed in moderation.
NECTARINE	vitamin **C, A**, potassium, niacin, copper	high in antioxidants, promotes better digestion, strengthens immune system, stabilizes blood sugar, improves heart health	Yes	High in tannins; great choice for daily use. Organic preferred as many pesticides/ herbicides used.

No Single fruit should be fed exclusively. Variety is the key.

FRUITS	NUTRIENTS	REPORTED BENEFITS	FREEZES WELL	COMMENTS
PALM FRUIT	vitamin **A, C, E**, B, **K**, potassium, calcium, iron, fiber, zinc, magnesium, phosphorous	facilitate smooth digestion, essential energy source, helps boost immune system, fibres present help control the blood sugar levels, stimulates growth of new skin cells	No	Rare and difficult to find. High in omega fatty acids.
PAPAYA	vitamin **C, A**, calcium, folate, magnesium, potassium, Beta-carotene, pantothenic acid, omega 3 fatty acids	potent antioxidant, anti-parasitic, good cleanser, soothes intestinal inflammation	No	Rich in vitamin C so use sparingly with iron sensitive individuals. Seeds are also safe to offer.
PASSION FRUIT	vitamin **A, C**, B6, iron, magnesium, potassium	rich source of antioxidants, good source of dietary fiber, may help reduce inflammation, aids in digestion, improves circulation	No	Source of phytonutrients, antioxidants; feed inside, not peel.
PEACH	vitamin **C, A**, potassium, magnesium, iron	combats free radicals, high antioxidant, anti-inflammatory and antifungal properties, treats gut disorders, destroys candida fungus	Yes	Unless organically grown, substitute nectarines, watermelon, and kiwis.
PEAR	vitamin **C, K**, calcium, magnesium, potassium, folic acid, iodine, pectine, copper, manganese	stimulates metabolism, pectin removes toxins from gut, high in fiber, high source of immune-boosting vitamin C, provides antioxidants	No	Great for daily use; some varieties may ripen faster than others, look for organically grown.
PEPINO MELON	vitamin **A**, C, K, protein, iron, copper, potassium, beta-carotene	lowers blood pressure, natural energy booster, excellent immunity booster, digestive benefits, rich in antioxidant phytochemicals	No	Moisture rich.
PINEAPPLE	vitamin **C**, B6, calcium, magnesium, potassium, folate, beta-carotene, high in fiber, **manganese**	antispasmodic, contains bromelain (good for digestion) clear bacteria and parasites, reduces inflammation, rich source of immune boosting vitamin C	No	Feed sparingly. Bromelain reportedly reduces inflammation and increases digestive functioning.
PLANTAINS	vitamin **C, A**, B6, potassium, iron, magnesium	great source of potassium, help regulate the digestive system, reduce the number of harmful free radicals, boost the immune system, great source of magnesium	Yes	Also known as cooking banana; green plantains must be cooked, ripe black plantains can be fed raw.

No Single fruit should be fed exclusively. Variety is the key.				
FRUITS	NUTRIENTS	REPORTED BENEFITS	FREEZES WELL	COMMENTS
PLUM YELLOW PLUM	vitamin **C, K, A,** E, B6, folate, manganese phosphorus, calcium, magnesium, iron, potassium	high source of antioxidants that helps prevent certain types of cell damage, especially those caused by oxidation, aids digestion, boosts immune system	No	Great choice for daily use when domestic available. Organic preferred.
POMEGRANATE	vitamin **C, K,** B6, potassium, folate, phosphorus	contain punicalagins, punicic acid, substances that are responsible for health benefits, potent anti-inflammatory properties, has anti-bacterial and anti-viral properties	Yes	Great for dietary enrichment; austerity food and great for adding to mashes.
RASPBERRY	vitamin **C, K,** E, **manganese,** folate, magnesium, iron, copper, high in fiber	can help manage diabetes, has anti-inflammatory	Yes	Difficult to keep; may fed defrosted. Use organic. Use in limited quantities.
RED CURRANTS	vitamin **C, K, iron, copper,** manganese	assist in red blood cell formation, improve digestive health and fight constipation	Yes	Can be fed raw or dried. A great addition to mashes.
STRAWBERRY	vitamin **C, A,** K, B6, **manganese,** folate, potassium, magnesium	rich in antioxidants, aids in detoxification	Yes	Unless organically grown, substitute blueberries, raspberries, watermelon and kiwis.
GUAVA	vitamin **C, A, fiber, lycopene,** folate, potassium, magnesium, phosphorus	boosts the immune system, great source of potassium for lowering blood pressure, more powerful antioxidants than almost any other fruit	No	Avoid common guava. High in vitamin C. Feed in limited quantities.
TAMARILLO	vitamin **A, C,** E, **phosphorus, potassium, manganese,** calcium, iron	promotes digestion, increase metabolism, reduce cholesterol, boost immunity, rejuvenate cells in the organs	Yes	Half fruit and scoop out flesh; tangy & mildly sweet. High in vitamin C. Use in limited quantities.
TANGERINE	vitamin **C, A,** B6, potassium, calcium, magnesium	rich antioxidants, prevents inflammation, absorbs iron from food, restricts cholesterol absorption, improves digestion, prevents chronic diseases, high fiber content eases bowel movements, enhances cell division	No	Acidic; feed in limited quantities.
WATERMELON	vitamin **C, A,** B1, B6, potassium, magnesium, copper, manganese, pantothenic acid	high antioxidant food, boosts immunity, helps manage high blood pressure and improves heart health, prevents kidney stones, detoxifies the body, anti-inflammatory	No	Moisture rich; use in smaller quantities.

		NO SINGLE HERB SHOULD BE FED EXCLUSIVELY. VARIETY IS THE KEY.		
HERBS	NUTRIENTS	REPORTED BENEFITS	FREEZES WELL	COMMENTS
BASIL	vitamin **A**, **K**, C, manganese	helps alkalize the body and improve digestion, has disease-fighting antioxidants, anti-inflammatory, antibacterial & antimicrobial properties, combats stress as an 'adaptogen'	No	Great addition to mashes.
CORIANDER (CILANTRO)	vitamin **A**, **K**, C, E, **potassium**, folate, calcium, iron, magnesium	strong antioxidant properties, expels heavy metals, settles digestive upset, prevents neurological inflammation, lowers blood sugar levels	No	Has natural antibacterial properties.
CEYLON cinnamon bark	vitamin K, E **potassium**, iron, calcium	high in anti-oxidant, anti-diabetic, anti-septic, and anti-inflammatory properties	No	Never offer Cassia Cinnamon due to high content of Coumarin.
CHAMOMILE	vitamin A, calcium, magnesium, potassium, fluoride, folate	improves digestion, has strong anti-inflammatory and pain-reducing abilities, high source of antioxidants	No	One of the most ancient and versatile medicinal herbs; great for the reduction of anxiety.
CLOVES	vitamin C, A, K, D, E, B6, B12, thiamin, calcium, iron, zinc, magnesium, sodium, phosphorous, folate potassium, riboflavin	antibacterial and anti-inflammatory properties, boosts the immune system	No	Contains eugenol, which has been reported to possess antiseptic properties.
DILL	vitamin **A**, **C**, manganese, folate, iron	lowers cholesterol, source of energy, aids in digestion, contains antimicrobial effects, protects against free radicals	No	Rich in flavonoids like quercetin that reportedly reduce inflammation and support cardiac health.
LAVENDER	calcium	full of phytochemicals & antioxidants, against anxiety, has calming effects	No	Great for the reduction of anxiety.
MINT	vitamin **A**, **C**, **calcium, iron, magnesium**	one of the highest antioxidant capacities, aids in digestion, prevents respiratory disorders	No	Mint is a calming and soothing herb.
OREGANO	thymol, carvacrol, vitamin **K**, **A**, **iron**, **manganese**, iron, fiber, **potassium**	antifungal, anti-septic and anti-bacterial	No	By adding it a fresh veg chop can prevent from microbial growth.
PARSLEY	vitamin **K**, **C**, **A**, **folate, iron**, calcium, magnesium, potassium	high source of flavonoid anti-oxidants, may help fight kidney stones, urinary tract infections and gallbladder infections, antibacterial and antifungal properties, improves digestion, has immune-boosting vitamin C, helps balance hormones	No	Contain oxalates, feed in moderation.

		No Single herb should be fed exclusively. Variety is the key.		
Herbs	**Nutrients**	**Reported Benefits**	**Freezes well**	**Comments**
Red Clover	vitamin **C**, calcium, chromium, magnesium, niacin, phosphorus, potassium, thiamine	helps maintain bone strength, treats skin inflammation, fights respiratory infections, has immune-boosting effects, helps fight inflammation, infections and hormonal imbalances	No	Contains isoflavones, becoming phytoestrogens after entering body. Beneficial phytoestrogens can functionally imitate the estrogen hormone in body.
Rosemary	vitamin **C, A, B6, calcium, iron**, magnesium, **potassium**	reduces inflammation, relieves pain, protects immune system, reduces stress & anxiety, protects from bacterial infections detoxifies, stimulates circulation	Yes	Great for including in mashes.
Sage	vitamin **A, C, B6**, folate, **calcium, magnesium, iron**, manganese, folic acid, thiamin, pyridoxine, riboflavin, **potassium**	natural antiseptic, preservative and bacteria-killing abilities	No	Supports digestive and metabolic health.
Star Anise	vitamin **C**, A, B6, **iron, calcium**, anethole, magnesium	kills bacteria, rich in antioxidants, wards off fungal infections, may boost heart health, natural flu fighter, helps regulate blood sugar	No	The entire pod should be offered as healthy compounds like shikimic acid are in the seed pod itself. Can be added to mashes.
Thyme	vitamin **C, A**, B6, iron, **manganese**, calcium, magnesium, riboflavin, copper, potassium	has antioxidant capacity, supports immune and digestive system	Yes	Contains compounds that support cardiovascular, respiratory and immune health.
Misc.	**Nutrients**	**Reported Benefits**	**Comments**	
Coconut Water	**magnesium**, zinc, **potassium**, folic acid, vitamin C, B6, riboflavin, calcium, iron, sodium, **manganese**	rehydrating, booster of energy, lowers blood pressure, reduces cholesterol and triglycerides, cleansing/detox, helps to replenish electrolytes, reduces stress and muscle tension	The clear liquid in raw coconut. High in potassium, making it a high electrolyte beverage. Sometimes confused with coconut milk that is higher in fat and calories. Coconut milk is extracted from the flesh of the coconut and is thicker and sweeter.	
Coconut Oil	source of lauric and fatty acid, and medium-chain triglycerides	act as antiviral, antibacterial and antifungal	Great energy source of medium chain triglycerides. Lauric acid also has reported antimicrobial benefits.	

Soaking and Sprouting:
Making nutrients more accessible BY DR. JASON CREAN

Feeding birds is certainly not an exact science for a plethora of reasons. There are many different species, each with potentially diverse needs, the changing needs of an individual bird over time, availability of different food items throughout a given year, and differences in the bioavailability of different food items often leave us scratching our heads. Research on the feeding of pet birds is lacking for many of the aforementioned reasons (Sales & Janssens, 2003). So how can we ensure our birds are not only getting the nutrients they need, but also nutrients that are available to the body in their unprocessed form? My philosophy has always been simple: feeding a diverse diet of whole foods can allow birds choice and is bound to cover the nutritional bases that are often unclear.

The basic needs are clear: birds require vitamins and minerals, as well as proteins, lipids (fats) and carbohydrates. They also need water, sometimes referred to a moisture, which can become available when items like carbohydrates, lipids and proteins are digested (Butcher & Miles, 2014). Many foods may appear to contain these nutrients, but whether they are truly in the food or accessible to the body can be a very different matter. For example, some rely more on the quantity of protein over the quality; if quality is low, the protein cannot be absorbed and utilized by the bird (Sales & Janssens, 2003). One fact remains, however: we can be confident as to what composes foods in their raw, whole form and that should form the basis of a diet. One of the greatest concerns voiced to me is

one of convenience. After all, is it not easier to simply leave a dry food out all day? Yes, but is that allowing our birds to thrive, or just survive? I would argue the latter, so having a system that works for the bird owner that allows for the feeding of fresh, unadulterated food is critical. I create mashes for my birds that allow for a great diversity of items that can be frozen and defrosted for convenience. I define a mash as a mixture of raw, fresh food items such as soaked and sprouted seeds and nuts, diced vegetables and certain fruits, as well as dried herbs and flowers to increase the diversity in colors and textures. Let us see how we can provide as much nutrition in a couple of spoonfuls of food to ensure our birds are receiving the basic nutrients their bodies need.

Fresh, whole foods like sprouts, vegetables and fruits are moisture-rich so a lack of water should never be an issue when offering these foods. And soaking and/or sprouting dry items such as grains, legumes, seeds and nuts not only infuses them with moisture, but also increases their digestibility and nutrient availability (Gupta, Gangoliya, & Singh, 2015).

One example which happens to be one of my favorite items to sprout is the mung bean, and the act of "germination resulted in a greater retention of all minerals compared to other processes" (Mubarak, 2005). Mashes that include these living plant-based foods can provide a host of different nutrients that are not only plentiful but also accessible to the body since they are in their unprocessed raw form.

Complete proteins can be accessed through these plant-based diets (McDougall, 2002). As amino acids are the building blocks of proteins, they are needed in the diet. Hemp and chia seeds, quinoa, almonds and sunflower seed can all provide valuable these valuable amino acids that cells can then use to assemble proteins. Soaking and/or sprouting these items makes these nutrients more available. Foods rich in healthy fats include walnuts and other tree nuts, flaxseed and hemp seed, and the oils made from these seeds.

Soaking is the simple process where the whole seed is soaked in clean water for a period of time that varies with the item. Soaking activates the growth process, in part, by allowing the diffusion of antinutrients and growth inhibiting chemicals out of the seed. These chemicals keep the seed from sprouting until environmental conditions are right. Sprouting follows the initial soak where the seed germinates and begins to develop differentiated plant structures like leaves and stems. This process is driven by enzymatic activity so feeding these sprouts during this process captures these proteins. After sprouting has begun, any item can be fed. Some items only require soaking to make them more digestible. Soaking seeds, grains, nuts or legumes in water for a period of time, and then sprouting allows the soaked item to germinate further. In other words, you first must soak something before you can sprout it. Most agree that soaking is a great first step towards good nutrition, but consensus is that foods which are soaked and then sprouted for a period of time become more nutrient dense during the growth process.

Taking a few days of food preparation can result in weeks to months of healthy raw foods for your birds. After soaking and/or sprouting the items discussed above and mixing them with diced vegetables, herbs, and flowers, I bag and freeze them into portions, only defrosting enough for a day or two at a time. According to Dr. Karen Becker, veterinarian and international authority of animal nutrition, freezing these foods may result in some lost nutrients but overall, preserves most of the benefits these foods provide. Any bird will consume these raw, whole foods; it entirely depends on your effort at persistence. Continue to offer foods, experimenting with different combinations until you find something that works for both you and your birds. Feeding these raw foods will continue to help you move bird from just surviving to thriving!

References

Butcher, G.D. & Miles, R.D. (Rev. 2014). Understanding pet bird nutrition. U.S. Departmentof Agriculture, UF/IFAS Extension Service, University of Florida, IFAS, Florida A & M University Cooperative Extension Program, and Boards of County Commissioners Cooperating. Gupta, R. K., Gangoliya, S. S., & Singh, N. K. (2015). Reduction of phytic acid and enhancement of bioavailable micronutrients in food grains. Journal of Food Science and Technology, 52(2), 676–684.

McDougall, J. (2002). Plants foods have a complete amino acid composition. Circulation, 105(25), 197.

Mubarak, A. E. (2005). Nutritional composition and antinutritional factors of mung bean seeds (Phaseolus aureus) as affected by some home traditional processes. Food Chemistry, 89(4), 489-495.

Sales, J. & Janssens, G. (2003). Energy and protein nutrition of companion birds. Vlaams Diergeneeskundig Tijdschrift (Flemish Veterinary Journal), 72(1), 51-58.

Soaking and Sprouting Schedule

RECOMMENDATIONS BY DR. JASON CREAN, AVIAN RAW WHOLE FOOD NUTRITION GROUP

For making a mash that can be frozen, soaking and sprouting is critical. For example, a sample schedule below may help you organize the items you soak and sprout based on the various lengths of time needed for each. Not all items need to be included but it helps to use the guide below for soaking times.

RINSING (INITIAL): All dry items should be rinsed before soaking.

SOAKING: Soaking in cool clean water at room temperature. Placing a stainless steel mesh strainer inside of a stainless steel mixing bowl allows for quick rinsing and replacing of soaking water and easy clean up.

RINSING (MAINTENANCE): Strain and rinse thoroughly. 20-25 drops Grapefruit Seed Extract per gallon of cool, clean water should be used as a dip or spray. Place in a fresh GSE-water mixture for a few minutes. Strain without rinsing and allow to sprout.

SPROUTING: Repeat the last step 2-3 times per day, always leaving the sprouts in a cool, dry place. You may refrigerate during the sprouting process which may slow it a bit.

Item	Soak Time	Sprout Time	Notes
GRAINS			
AMARANTH	2-4 HOURS	1-1.5 DAYS	
BARLEY	6-8 HOURS	2 DAYS	PEARLED BARLEY MAY NOT SPROUT AS IT HAS BEEN PROCESSED TO REMOVE ITS HULL AND BRAN. USE UNHULLED BARLEY AS EVEN "WHOLE" HULLED BARLEY MAY NOT SPROUT. IT MAY BE SOAKED AND FED HOWEVER.
BUCKWHEAT	15 MINUTES	1-2 DAYS	
FIELD CORN	8-14 HOURS	2+ DAYS	
KAMUT	8-14 HOURS	1-1.5 DAYS	
MILLET	8 HOURS	2-3 DAYS	UNHULLED MILLET IS THE BEST SPROUTER.
OATS	8-14 HOURS	1-1.5 DAYS	MUST USE UNHULLED OATS. SO-CALLED "WHOLE OATS" OR OAT GROATS MAY NOT SPROUT.
QUINOA (WHITE, RED, BLACK)	2 HOURS	1-2 DAYS	RINSE THOROUGHLY TO REMOVE SAPONIN.
RYE	8-14 HOURS	1-1.5 DAYS	WARNING! WATCH FOR ERGOT MOLD
SPELT	8-14 HOURS	1-1.5 DAYS	
TEFF	2 HOURS	1 DAY	
WHEAT GRAIN	7 HOURS	2-3 DAYS	

Item	Soak Time	Sprout Time	Notes
LEGUMES			
Adzuki beans	8 hours	3-5 days	
Alfalfa	4-14 hours	1-1.5 days	
Clover	4-14 hours	1-1.5 days	
Garbanzo beans (chickpeas)	12 hours	12 hours	
Lentils (brown/green/red)	8 hours	12 hours	
Mung beans	1 day	2-5 days	
Peas (whole)	12 hours	2-3 days	Split peas won't sprout but are still suitable for soaking.
Nuts & Seeds			
Almonds (hulled)	8-12 hours	12 hours	
Cashew	2.5 hours	N/A	
Flax seeds	8 hours	N/A	
Fenugreek seeds	8 hours	2-3 days	
Mustard Seeds	6 hours	1+ Days	Yellow or black are recommended.
Pecan (hulled)	4-6 hours	N/A	
Pepita (pumpkin seeds)	6-8 hours	1-2 days	
Poppy seeds	8 hours	1-2 days	
Sesame seeds	8 hours	1-2 days	Must use unhulled sesame seeds for sprouting. Sesame sprouts can be fed immediately after soaking but continue to grow while refrigerated.
Sunflower Seeds	2 hours	2-3 days	Hulled or unhulled may be soaked and sprouted.
Walnut (hulled)	4 hours	N/A	

The Importance of Morning Meals

In the wild, a parrot's diet is as complex and varied as is the regions they all live in. Food sources can be diverse. When we bring parrots into our homes, diets can be a lot of things, but should never be boring. Unexciting meals mean your birds are only eating to alleviate their hunger and could also be preventing them from receiving the nutrition they need. One of the secrets to preventing health issues in parrots is to provide a healthy, balanced diet. Make it exciting, and colorful, but most important, give them the variety they require to cover all their nutritional needs.

Wild parrots can fly many miles to forage for a food source each day. Our pet parrots get 'room service', then take a little snooze. As terrific as that lifestyle might sound, too much food and not enough activity can be unhealthy for our birds.

In the wild, birds fly off in search of their first meal at daybreak so it's very important to include their most nutritious meal first thing in the morning when they are the hungriest. The early afternoon hours are usually spent preening, playing, napping, and bathing. Afterward, they feed again, then return to their home for the night.

As their caregivers, we must fit their feedings around our schedules, but try to stick to the two most nutritional meals in the day—morning and night.

Nothing substitutes vitamins, proteins, and nutrients found in fresh, green, raw, organic LIVE foods. They carry the ability of life itself.

Remember the old saying
"You are what you eat"
also applies to our feathered friends too!

Go Organic!

Organic refers to food grown without the use of pesticides, artificial fertilizers, sewage sludge, bioengineering, or ionizing radiation.

Parrots are known to be quite sensitive to certain ingredients in foods, hence we believe that by providing organically grown vegetables and fruits, you can prevent potential allergies, neurological problems, hormonal imbalances, and disruptions of their fragile immune systems that may be attributed directly to pesticide residues from non-organic food. Most organically grown fruit and vegetables can be given to your bird with its skin on; but if you offer non-organic foods, remember to remove the skin or soak and wash very thoroughly with vegetable washes to remove pesticides and toxins.

SIZE MATTERS FOR PICKY EATERS

Each bird has its preference, but since parrots can be picky eaters, cutting food into small pieces and mixing everything together will help them to ingest a variety of good nutrition. This is also helpful when trying to introduce new foods. Almost all parrots seem to like mashed yams or sweet potatoes. You can use these foods as a base to introduce new foods and mix them all together. This is also a great way to get them off a seed diet.

If you have a fussy eater that is refusing vegetables, just be persistent and offer a different variety of foods daily. Persistence is the key. Sometimes it can take months before your bird finally gets its beak into it, especially when transitioning from an exclusive seed or pellet diet, but it's worth it.

**GET CREATIVE!
IT'S ALL ABOUT THE PRESENTATION!**

Nutritional Tip:

If you are new to the soaking and sprouting process, then it's beneficial to read about soaking and sprouting in the chapter titled: 'Soaking and Sprouting Schedule' by Dr. Jason Crean, on page 53 before making any of these mashes and chops.

By adding herbs and spices like fresh oregano or rosemary to fresh foods, you can prevent potential spoilage. Using herbs can deter microbial growth, as the additions contain compounds like thymol and carvacrol that are well studied antimicrobial agents. Raw coconut oil is another option to use. See chapter 'Evening Meals' on page 79 for more details about raw coconut oil.

Good to Know: Sprouting seeds burns off the fat found in seed that gives the seed the energy to turn into a plant. Once the fat is burned off, it is transformed into a live and highly nutritious food that is rich in vitamins and minerals as well as enzymes and antioxidants. So even the unpopular sunflower seeds then become very nutritious.

It is best to buy organic seeds, legumes and nuts that are human grade.

Commercially produced seed mixes are usually dusty and bulked up with high fat seeds like sunflowers or peanuts that are deficient in calcium, vitamin A, and other nutrients.

If these mixes are fed exclusively, your bird could develop serious and life-threatening illnesses. Birds will usually pick through a large bowl of commercial seed mix and selectively eat 1 or 2 favorite types of seeds, limiting their nutrient intake even further. That's why it is so important to offer seeds in a soaked or sprouted form to maximize their nutritional value.

Safety Tip: *Soup-type beans are not safe to soak and sprout. The only safe way to offer those is in a cooked form, which then has no nutritional value for the bird. The only safe beans that can be sprouted and soaked are adzuki, mung and garbanzos (chickpeas), along with other legumes like lentils and peas.*

Always remove any uneaten vegetable or fruit chop after 4 hours to avoid spoilage and bacterial growth.

DR. JASON CREAN'S SPECIAL MASH

ITEM	SOAK TIME	SPROUT TIME	START DAY
Sunflower	2-4 hours	2-3 days	Day 1 (morning)
Pepita (green pumpkin)	6-8 hours	1-2 days	Day 1 (morning)
Wheat	7-8 hours	2-3 days	Day 1 (morning)
Lentils	8 hours	12 hours	Day 1 (morning)
Fenugreek	8 hours	3-5 days	Day 1 (morning)
Millet	8 hours	2-3 days	Day 1 (morning)
Peas	12-24 hours	2-3 days	Day 1 (morning)
Garbanzo	12-24 hours	12 hours	Day 1 (morning)
Mung	24 hours	2-5 days	Day 1 (morning)
Buckwheat	15 minutes	1-2 days	Day 2 (morning)
Quinoa	2-4 hours	1-2 days	Day 2 (morning)
Sesame	8 hours	1-2 days	Day 2 (morning)
Poppy	8 hours	1-2 days	Day 2 (morning)
Cashew	2.5 hours	N/A	Day 2 (night)
Walnut	4-6 hours (overnight)	N/A	Day 2 (night)
Pecan	4-6 hours (overnight)	N/A	Day 2 (night)
Barley	6-8 hours (overnight)	2 days	Day 2 (night)
Almond	7-8 hours (overnight)	12 hours	Day 2 (night)
Split peas	7-8 hours (overnight)	12 hours	Day 2 (night)

INSTRUCTIONS

Once all of these listed seeds from the table are soaked and/or sprouted per their specific time periods, we add dry items like the tea blends that include dried flowers, rolled oats and other grains, shredded unsweetened coconut, Ceylon cinnamon, anise seed pods, dry shelled nuts, etc to a large mixing bin.

We then add various diced vegetables and even cranberries or pomegranate when in season. We bag up enough for 2-3 days of use at a time which is stored in the refrigerator after it has been defrosted.

PREPARING MASH: A DAY-BY-DAY GUIDE

Day 1: I begin by soaking items that require a significant amount of time to sprout to ensure they will be ready by the end of our 3-day process.

I place these in their own individual stainless-steel mesh strainers, rinse well, and then submerge the entire strainer and its contents in cool clean water on a counter at room temperature. Items that require the longest soaking times include garbanzo (chickpeas), mung beans, and whole peas. Items that follow this same day include pepitas (green pumpkin seeds), wheat, lentils, hulled sunflower, and fenugreek.

If any of these have similar soaking times, like sunflower and wheat, I soak and sprout them together. After each item is done soaking, I thoroughly rinse, dip the entire strainer and its contents in the GSE water, and then strain and let sit at room temperature. I rinse 2-3 times daily, always dipping in the GSE solution so that it remains on the items as they sprout.

Day 2: I begin soaking the next round of items including quinoa, sesame, and buckwheat. I follow the same directions as in Day 1 after the initial soak is complete for each item. At night, I soak the items that will only need to soak overnight. These include nuts, split peas, and any grains like barley.

Day 3: I rinse all items and allow them to sit and dry a bit in their strainers while I prepare the vegetables. In a large bin where I mix all contents, I add the dry items that include dried flowers, rolled oats and other grains, shredded unsweetened coconut, Ceylon cinnamon, anise seed pods, dry shelled nuts (diced), etc. I then add diced vegetables, both leafy and otherwise, throwing them on top of the dry items. Finally, I add the soaked and sprouted items and mix all contents together. This mash is then bagged up for freezing or feeding.

Salads, Chops and Mashes

Fresh vegetables are the best way to enhance your bird's diet. Also, by adding sprouts or soaked seeds, you can really make a big difference in your bird's daily nutrition intake. Parrots also love their fruits; however, those higher in sugar should be fed in moderation.

RAINBOW MASH

INGREDIENTS
Handful of microgreens
1/4 cup green squash,
  finely chopped
1/4 cup kale, finely chopped
1 carrot, grated
1/2 red bell pepper,
   finally chopped
1 tbsp buckwheat flakes
1 tbsp dry organic rose hips
1 pansy flower (Viola),
   to garnish (optional)
1 sprig of fresh rosemary,
   to garnish
1 tbsp avian herbal tea, Golden Blossom,
from Polly's Natural Parrot Boutique
 (optional)

Sprouted
1 tbsp white quinoa
1 tbsp peas
1 tbsp sunflower seeds
1 tbsp chickpeas (garbanzo beans)
1 tbsp fenugreek seeds
1 tbsp mung beans

Soaked
1 tbsp barley
1 tbsp pecans, roughly chopped

Nutrition Tip: *Sprouting burns off the fat found in a seed that gives it the energy to turn into a plant. Once the fat is burned off it is transformed into a live and highly nutritious food.*

INSTRUCTIONS

Soak and sprout all the listed ingredients.

Finely chop all the vegetables, add buckwheat flakes, rose hips and toss all gently together.

To finish, sprinkle with Polly's organic herbal tea mix, fresh rosemary, and flowers.

*Polly's Natural Parrot Boutique Tea is only available outside of the U.S.

SUPERPOWER MASH

INGREDIENTS

1/4 cup pumpkin, grated
1/4 cup red cabbage
1/4 cup green beans
2 tbsp microgreens
1/4 cup sugar snap peas
1 sprig of dill, chopped
1 tbsp flax seeds
2 dianthus or pansy flowers (optional)
2 star anise (optional)
1 tbsp avian herbal tea, Nature Boost,
from Polly's Natural Parrot Boutique (optional)

Sprouted
1 tbsp brown lentils
1 tbsp mung beans
1 tbsp kamut grain
1 tbsp milk thistle seeds

Soaked
1 tbsp amaranth grain
1 tbsp teff
2 tbsp oat groats
1 tbsp millet grain
2 tbsp sesame seeds
1 tbsp almonds

INSTRUCTIONS

Soak and sprout all the listed ingredients. Finely chop all the vegetables and gently toss all the ingredients together.

To finish, sprinkle with *Polly's organic herbal tea mix, flax seeds, finely chopped dill, a few star anise pods, and flowers.

*TEA FROM POLLY'S NATURAL PARROT BOUTIQUE IS ONLY AVAILABLE OUTSIDE OF THE U.S.

RED BEET MINI SALAD

INGREDIENTS

1x raw beet, grated
1x carrot
1/2 cup baby spinach
1/4 cucumber
1/4 tsp palm oil
1 tbsp raw corn
1 sprig of dill, to garnish
1 tsp flax seeds, to garnish

Sprouted
1 tbsp mung beans

INSTRUCTIONS

Grate raw beet and slice the carrot to small strips then chop the cucumber to small cubes. Place it all in a medium size bowl together with chopped spinach and corn.

Drizzle with palm oil, add in the sprouted mung beans and toss gently, sprinkle with flax seeds, and decorate with piece of fresh dill.

GREEN MASH

INGREDIENTS
1 tbsp cooked organic brown rice
1/4 cucumber
Handful of kale
1 chili pepper
1 sprig of fresh thyme
1 tbsp white cabbage
1 tbsp curly parsley
Handful of watercress, to garnish

Sprouted
1 tbsp mung beans
1 tbsp fenugreek seeds
1 tbsp barley (unhulled)
1 tbsp red clover seeds
1 tbsp chickpeas (garbanzo beans)

Soaked
1 tbsp pepitas
1 tbsp sesame
1 tbsp almonds

INSTRUCTIONS

Place the cucumber, kale, chili pepper, cabbage, and thyme in a food processor and coarsely chop.

Then combine brown rice and water in a pot and bring to a boil. Reduce heat, cover, and simmer until tender. Cool it in cold water right after cooking and drain. Mix with the vegetable mix, sprouts, and seeds.

Lay the watercress in the bottom of a small bowl and place the entire mix on top. Season with finely chopped curly parsley and almonds.

Safety Tip: *Brown rice can go bad quickly. Be sure to refrigerate and do not leave in their bowls longer than 90 minutes.*

STUFFED ARTICHOKE FORAGING TREAT

INGREDIENTS

1 organic large artichoke
1/4 red bell pepper
1 carrot
1 radish
1 sprig of thyme, to garnish
1 raw fig
1 tbsp crushed Brazil nuts

INSTRUCTIONS

Rinse artichoke well, tugging leaves outward to loosen slightly for stuffing. Cut all the vegetables into long chunky strips and stuff under each leaf starting from the bottom and working your way around.

Sprinkle crushed Brazil nuts inside the artichoke or you can hide them inside as whole. This will definitely keep your feathered friend occupied for some time.

Tip: *This can be great as a foraging "treat" with plenty to eat, too, and you can fit as many different ingredients in as you can.*

CRUNCHY MONDAY CHOP

INGREDIENTS

1/4 cup watercress
1/2 cup broccoli, chopped
1/4 cucumber
1 okra
2 raw baby sweetcorn
1/2 carrot, ribbons
1 tbsp pomegranate seeds
1/2 tbsp hazelnuts
1 tbsp fresh cranberries
1 tsp dry organic oregano
1 tbsp parsley, finely chopped
1 tsp chia seeds, to garnish

Sprouted
1 tbsp mung beans

Soaked
1 tbsp buckwheat
1 tbsp teff seeds
1 tbsp sesame seeds

INSTRUCTIONS

Chop the watercress, broccoli, cucumber, okra, and baby sweetcorn, and place them into a bowl. Add whole fresh cranberries, crushed hazelnuts, sprouted mung beans and pomegranate seeds.

Next, layer on the soaked seeds and gently toss. To finish it off, sprinkle with chia seeds, dry oregano, fresh parsley and carrot ribbons.

SWEET POWER CHOP

INGREDIENTS

1/4 cup plantain, diced (must be ripped if
    served raw, otherwise must be cooked)
1/2 cup courgette (zucchini)
1 cup dandelion greens
2 brussels sprouts
1/2 cup sweetcorn, raw
1 tbsp pomegranate seeds
1 sprig of fresh coriander, to garnish

Sprouted
1/4 cup red quinoa
1 tbsp chickpeas (garbanzo beans)

Soaked
1 tsp cashew nuts, roughly chopped

INSTRUCTIONS

Cut the plantain into small cubes, place them into steamer basket and cover. Remove once tender, drain, and let it cool.

Chop all the other ingredients into smaller pieces, add sprouts, soaked cashews, and toss gently. Sprinkle with finely chopped coriander and pomegranate seeds.

Safety Tip:
Never offer your bird salted cashews.

SWEET POTATO COUSCOUS SALAD

INGREDIENTS

1 cup couscous, cooked
1/4 cup sweet potato, gently steamed
1/2 green or red bell pepper
2 tbsp kale
1 tbsp pomegranate seeds
1 tbsp fresh curly parsley

Sprouted

1 tbsp alfalfa
1 tbsp fenugreek seeds
1 tbsp rye grain

Soaked

1 tbsp almonds, chopped

INSTRUCTIONS

Use a ratio of 1-1/2 cups of water per 1 cup of couscous. Bring the water to a boil. Pour the boiling water over the couscous, cover and let sit for 5 to 10 minutes. Once ready place it in a bowl. All water should have been absorbed.

Meanwhile, peel and cut the sweet potato into medium cubes, place them into steamer basket, and cover. Remove from steamer when tender and let it cool. Finely chop the pepper and kale then gently mix with couscous, sprouts, and soaked, chopped almonds. Garnish with parsley, pomegranate seeds, and sweet potato.

FRUIT SKEWERS WITH PASSION FRUIT & MANGO SAUCE

INGREDIENTS

Green grapes
Blueberries
Kiwi slices, skinless
Watemelon
Apple, skinless and seedless

Sauce

1 passion fruit
1 slice of mango
1 tbsp chia seeds

Prep Tip: *Adjust the amount of ingredients depending on the number of skewers you will be making.*

INSTRUCTIONS

Wash and slice all fruit except the grapes. Thread the fruit onto skewers in the order you desire.

Place on the plate or their favourite bowl, and drizzle with blended mango and passion fruit sauce.

WRAP IT ALL UP WITH HUMMUS DIP

INGREDIENTS - MAIN

1 carrot
3 courgettes (zucchini), ribbons
1/4 red bell pepper
1/4 yellow bell pepper
3 sugar snap peas
3 sprigs of thyme

INSTRUCTIONS - MAIN

Cut the carrot and peppers into long thin strips. With vegetable peeler, slice courgette (zucchini) lengthwise into ribbons. Stop when you get to the seeded core.

Lay three ribbons in a single layer individually on the plate and place the carrot, pepper strips and sugar snap peas on to each ribbon and roll it up.

Garnish with sprig of thyme.

Those little feathered monsters will love unwrapping them while munching.

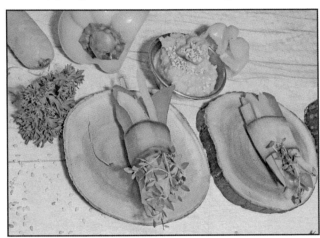

...CHICKPEA HUMMUS DIP

INGREDIENTS - DIP

1 cup chickpeas (garbanzo beans), steamed
1 slice of butternut squash, steamed
1/2 chili pepper
1 tbsp sesame seeds, to garnish

INSTRUCTIONS - DIP

Steam the chickpeas and butternut squash until tender enough to break up easily.

Drain the cooking liquid and let it cool, but keep the liquid. Then blend all in food processor until thick paste forms, and add uncooked sesame seeds and finely chopped chili pepper.

If the mixture is too thick, add water a teaspoon at a time. Garnish with small slices of chili pepper and sesame seeds.

69

STUFFED PEPPER

INGREDIENTS
1 large bell pepper
1 tbsp organic brown rice, cooked
1/4 cucumber
Handful of kale
1 chili pepper
2 tbsp white cabbage
4 green beans
1 tbsp coriander (cilantro)
1 tbsp macadamia nuts, crushed
Handful of watercress, to garnish

Sprouted
1 tbsp mung beans
1 tbsp fenugreek seeds
1 tbsp barley (unhulled)
1 tbsp red clover seeds
1 tbsp chickpeas (garbanzo beans)

Soaked
1 tbsp pepitas
1 tbsp sesame seeds
1 tbsp almonds

INSTRUCTIONS

Cut the top of the bell pepper and remove seeds. Keep the top part aside for later.

Meanwhile, combine brown rice and water in a pot and bring to a boil. Reduce heat, cover and simmer until tender. Cool in cold water and drain well.

Place the cucumber, kale, chili pepper, and cabbage in a food processor and coarsely chop. In a small bowl, mix all the ingredients for the stuffing, including cooked rice, sprouts, and soaked seeds. Season with finely chopped coriander.

Fill the pepper with stuffing and serve it on a bed of watercress with green beans on side, sprinkle with crushed macadamia nuts. Cover the pepper with the previously cut top.

Your bird will enjoy trying to get through it.

COURGETTINI

INGREDIENTS
1 cup courgette (zucchini)
1 cup yellow squash, finely chopped
5 sugar snap peas, chopped
1 tbsp pomegranate seeds
2 tbsp watercress salad microgreens
1/4 beet, grated
2 tbsp coriander (cilantro), to garnish

Sprouted
1 tbsp oat (unhulled)
1 tbsp milk thistle seeds
1 tbsp red clover seeds
1 tbsp sesame seeds
1 tbsp amaranth
1 tbsp adzuki beans

Soaked
1 tbsp black quinoa
1 tbsp sunflower seeds
1 tbsp barley groats
1 tbsp yellow split peas

INSTRUCTIONS

Using a spiraliser or similar attachment, cut the courgette into strips and place it into a bowl.

Add all the other finely chopped/grated vegetables. Toss gently and add watercress microgreens, sprouts, soaked seeds, and sprinkle with pomegranate seeds.

To finish it off, garnish with a sprig of coriander.

BE MY VALENTINE KABOBS

INGREDIENTS
1/4 banana, peeled and sliced
    into 1/2 inch thick rounds
1 organic strawberry, whole
1 tbsp chia seeds
2 tbsp coconut flour

INSTRUCTIONS

Cut the banana into thick rounds and thread a strawberry piece, followed by a banana piece onto skewers.

Roll them in coconut flour.

Prep Tip: *Adjust the amount of ingredients depending on the number of skewers you will be making.*

SUMMER FRUIT SALAD IN COCONUT

INGREDIENTS
1 raw, whole coconut, cut in half
1 raw fig
1/4 pepino melon
2 organic strawberries
4 grapes
1/2 nectarine
1 tbsp almonds, soaked
1 tbsp raw cranberries, cut in half
1 tsp chia seeds
2 sprig of fresh mint, 1 finely chopped
1 physalis, to garnish

INSTRUCTIONS

Cut the coconut in half. Save the coconut water for your bird, they love it! It's refreshing and full of nutrition. Cut all the fruit into small pieces and place into one half of the coconut.

Add in almonds, sprinkle with chia seeds and finely chopped mint. Garnish with physalis and sprig of mint.

This can be great as foraging and introduction to fruits for your bird.

Safety Tip*: Remove the pit from nectarine as this is toxic to birds.*

COMBINATION OF RAW AND COOKED FOODS

The main 'meal' of the day is to be fed about two hours after your bird's wake up time in the morning. At least half of the meal will be consumed in about 15 minutes, with the remainder of dry pelleted food being consumed throughout the day. The rest of the diet is offered in the form of various treats that are fed sporadically.

Raw vegetable salads, chops, and mashes should always be considered a parrot's main meal. Any cooked food should be fed sparingly.

POLLY'S MINIATURES COCONUT PANCAKES WITH FRUIT TOPPING

INGREDIENTS

1/2 banana

1 free range egg

1/4 cup coconut flour

1 sprig of fresh mint

1 tsp chia seeds

1 tbsp raw coconut oil

Topping

2 tbsp blueberries

1 tbsp raspberries

1 tsp chia seeds

INSTRUCTIONS

Peel the banana and break it into several big chunks in a bowl. Use a dinner fork to mash the banana thoroughly. Continue mashing until the banana has a pudding-like consistency and no large lumps remain.

Whisk the egg together until the yolk and white is completely combined. Pour the egg over the banana and stir until the mix is completely combined, then add coconut flour.

The batter should not be liquidy, add more flour if required. Heat a lightly oiled frying pan over very low heat. Drop roughly 2 tablespoons of the batter onto the hot pan. (Remember still on very low heat)

Cook the pancakes until the bottoms look golden when you lift a corner. The edges should also be starting to look set. Flip the pancakes. Gently work a spatula about halfway under the pancake, then lift until the unsupported half of the pancake is just barely lifted off the skillet. Lay the pancake back down on its other side.

Cook the pancake for another minute or so, until the other side is also light golden color. You can flip the pancakes a few times if you need to in order to get them evenly browned.

Transfer the cooked pancakes to a serving plate/bowl and drizzle with raw fruit sauce and sprinkle with chia seeds. Garnish with sprig of fresh mint.

POACHED EGG AND SPINACH - BEET SALAD

INGREDIENTS

1 free range egg

1 sprig of dill

1 tsp flax seeds

Handful of spinach

1/2 raw beet

1 tsp raw peas

1 tbsp avian herbal tea, Nature Boost, from Polly's Natural Parrot Boutique (optional)

Sprouted

1 tbsp mug beans

1 tsp kamut seeds

1 tsp fenugreek seeds

INSTRUCTIONS

How to poach an egg

Fill a small pan just over one third full of cold water and bring it to a boil. Then turn down and let it simmer. Crack the egg into a small bowl and gently tip into the simmering water. Lightly poach for 5 minutes. **Make sure the yolk is well cooked and not runny!** Remove with a slotted spoon and drain on kitchen towel.

BEET SALAD

INSTRUCTIONS

Dice the peeled beet into small cubes, add spinach, sprouts, raw peas and finely chopped dill. Sprinkle with flax seeds and *Polly's organic herbal tea.

*TEA FROM POLLY'S NATURAL PARROT BOUTIQUE IS ONLY AVAILABLE OUTSIDE OF THE U.S.

ALMOND MINI PANCAKES

INGREDIENTS

1/2 banana

1/4 cup almond flour

1 tbsp hazelnuts, crushed

1 tbsp raw coconut oil

Toppings

1 passion fruit

2 organic strawberries

1 tsp rolled oats

OR

1/4 cup mango

1/2 pear

1 sprig fresh mint, finely chopped

Nutritional Tip: *In the wild, some birds tend to eat the eggs of other birds if they can find them and these can be very nutritious. The protein found in an egg is a valuable ingredient because it contributes amino acids to help brain function and liver funtion. Birds can eat the the white, yolk, as well as the shell. Of course, eggs served in our households must be served cooked.*

Eggs are good for your birds, but as with anything, moderation is key to a healthy flock.

Tip: *Always fry on a very low heat.*

INSTRUCTIONS

Peel the banana and break it up into several big chunks in a bowl. Use a dinner fork to thoroughly mash the banana. Continue mashing until the banana has a pudding-like consistency and no large lumps remain. Combine with almond flour then add crushed hazelnuts and mix it well.

Heat a lightly oiled frying pan over very low heat. Drop roughly 2 tablespoons of batter onto the hot pan. (Remember, still on low heat.)

Cook the pancakes until the bottoms look golden when you lift a corner. The edges should also be starting to look set. Flip the pancakes. Gently work a spatula about halfway under the pancake, then lift until the unsupported half of the pancake is just barely lifted off the skillet. Lay the pancake back down on its other side.

Cook the pancake for another minute or so, until the other side is also light gold. You can flip the pancakes a few times if you need to in order to get them evenly browned.

Transfer the cooked pancakes to a serving plate/bowl and drizzle with raw fruit sauce.

QUINOA, BANANA & POMEGRANATE "PORRIDGE"

INGREDIENTS

1/4 cup white quinoa, cooked
  (can also be offered soaked or sprouted)

1/4 banana

2 tbsp rolled oats

1 tbsp ceylon cinnamon stick, crushed

1 tbsp pomegranate seeds

Soaking

1 tbsp millet

2 tbsp walnuts, finely crushed

INSTRUCTIONS

To cook quinoa, rinse it first under cold running water. Put it in pan with water over medium heat and bring to a boil. Reduce to a simmer for 10 to 15 minutes, or until tender and the liquid is absorbed. Once cooked, let it cool down then place it into a bowl and add mashed banana. If consistency is too thick, add two tablespoons of boiled water.

Add remaining ingredients oats, cinnamon, and millet. Garnish with pomegranate seeds and walnuts.

GREEN VEGGIE OMELETTE

INGREDIENTS

1 free range egg

1 tbsp fresh sugar snap peas

1 tbsp red bell pepper, finely chopped

1 tbsp courgette (zucchini), finely chopped

1 tbsp flax seeds

1 tbsp pepita seeds

1 chili pepper

1 sprig of dill

1 tbsp raw coconut oil

1/2 pak choi (bok choy)

INSTRUCTIONS

Melt the raw coconut oil in a frying pan over very low heat. Add the finely chopped pepper, courgette, and chili pepper and cook gently on low heat for about 5 min. While the vegetables are cooking, beat the egg until frothy. Pour the egg mixture over the cooked vegetable evenly and allow to cook.

Sprinkle with some flax seeds. When the base firms up, flip it to the other side and cook it, then sprinkle with pepita seeds. Leave it to cool down before serving to your bird. Garnish with sugar snap peas and half cut pack choi and dill.

Evening meals

The evening meal is quite important to your bird. Always feed your parrot in the evening, no later than an hour before bedtime. A parrot that does not eat before bedtime may become restless and uncomfortable during the night.

Nutrition Tip: *When opting for frozen vegetables in your chops or mashes, always check their labels for added sodium or preservatives. These type of vegetables are not safe for parrots.*

Most companies use blanching to process their vegetables. This is a process of exposing them to boiling water or steam for a short period of time. This process removes any dirt but also destroys enzymes and breaks down nutrients.

Shopping Tip: Coconut Oil

Coconut oil is wonderful for parrots. When shopping for good quality, raw coconut oil always look for a brand that is cold pressed, non-GMO, organic, extra virgin, unrefined, unbleached, and hexane-free to ensure it is the healthiest for your bird companion. Coconut oil is easy to digest and good for allergies. It is also good topically for abraisions or dry skin. Contains lauric acid, which acts as an antiviral, antibacterial and antifungal.

PARROT RAW 'BURGER' WITH BUTTERNUT SQUASH CHIPS

INGREDIENTS

2 fennel slices

1 slice butternut squash

2 slices cucumber

1 slice yellow bell pepper

1 slice red bell pepper

1 slice red cabbage

2 spinach leaves

1 slice raw beet

1 slice radish, to garnish

The end of the green pepper, to garnish

Raw butternut squash, cut into chips of desired quantity

INSTRUCTIONS

Cut the fennel bulb in half lengthwise and peel off the outer layers. Put two of them aside.

Then cut all the other ingredience into thin round slices or use a round cookie cutter. To assemble the burger, place one fennel slice at the bottom and layer all the other vegetables on top of each other and finish with the second fennel slice.

Put small slice of radish and end of the pepper on top. To help hold the burger, pierce it all the way through with a bamboo skewer.

Tip: *Always use fresh vegetables. You can add or substitute any of the ingredients as long as it fits into the bird's safe food category.*

THE GREAT CHUNKY CHOP

INGREDIENTS

1/4 cup chopped kale

2 tbsp spinach

1/4 yellow squash

1/4 cup carrots, cut as ribbons

1 bell pepper

1/4 cup sugar snap peas

1/4 cup sweet potato,
  lightly steamed

2 tbsp shredded coconut

1 tbsp dry oregano

Edible flowers are optional. Use
  Nasturtiums, Calendula or Chamomile

Soaking

1 tbsp pecan nuts

1 tbsp almonds

1 tbsp black quinoa

1 tbsp amaranth

1 tbsp pepitas

INSTRUCTIONS

Soak all the listed ingredients.

Meanwhile cut the sweet potato in larger cubes and place them into steamer basket and cover. Remove once tender, drain, and let cool.

Roughly chop all the vegetables and combine all ingredients together.

Suitable for beaks that prefer chunky chop to a mash.

Safety Tip: *When buying flowers, ensure they are edible, organically grown, and suitable for human consumption, unless you are growing your own. Flowers from garden centers, nurseries, supermarkets, and florists are designed to be looked at, not eaten. They are sprayed with insecticides and fungicides which are absolutely not safe for your bird. Always ensure that the flower is on a safe bird food list.*

CAULIFLOWER-LENTIL CROQUETTES WITH SALAD

INGREDIENTS

1/4 cup cauliflower, steamed

1/4 cup chopped swede, steamed

2 tbsp brown lentils, cooked

2 tbsp barley flour

1 free range egg

1 tbsp fresh coriander (cilantro)

1 tbsp raw coconut oil

1 tsp sesame seeds

1 tsp flax seeds, to garnish

Soaked

1 tsp millet seeds

1 tbsp pecan nuts, whole or
   roughly chopped

Salad

1 chili pepper

3 florets of broccoli

1 tbsp raw corn

INSTRUCTIONS

Place cauliflower and swede in a steamer basket, set over water and steam for 7–10 minutes or until tender, then cool. Mash it all lightly with a fork, add cooked lentils, finely chopped coriander, and sesame seeds. Mix it well.

Make evenly-sized small 'sausages' with the croquette mixture, roll and coat them in barley flour, then in the egg, and fry them in pan on very low heat for 10 minutes. Cook until golden. Ensure they are thoroughly cooked on each side, then transfer onto paper towel.

Place on washed savoy cabbage leaf and sprinkle with flax seeds and chopped pecan nuts.

One 'sausage' is plenty for a parrot.

For salad, chop all the ingredients and add soaked millet. Toss and serve it in a bowl.

POLLY'S MINIATURE PIZZA

INGREDIENTS

Dough

1/4 cup sweet potato, diced and steamed

1/4 cup buckwheat flour

1 tsp raw coconut oil

Toppings

1/2 beet

2 tbsp shredded carrots

1 tbsp red bell pepper, finely diced

1/2 scotch bonnet chili pepper

1 tsp raw sweetcorn

2 spinach leaves

1 tbsp pepitas

...QUICK SALAD

INGREDIENTS

1/4 cup cucumber, diced

1 okra, diced

2-3 sugar snaps, chopped

1 tsp baby sweetcorn

1 radish, sliced

1 sprig of thyme, to garnish

INSTRUCTIONS

Preheat the oven to 170 C/350 F.

For dough: steam sweet potato until soft. In a bowl, mash up the sweet potato with a fork and mix with buckwheat flower. Knead the dough with your hands, soaking up the extra flour at the bottom of the bowl as you go. If the dough is still too wet add a touch of flour and knead again.

Shape dough into a small ball. Flour a rolling pin. Roll the dough all directions into a circular shape approx. 5 cm / 2 inches in diameter. It's fine if it's not a perfect circle. You can use a cookie cutter or a glass to cut small round shapes out of the dough. Place on parchment paper on a baking tray.

Drizzle with melted coconut oil and bake for about 10 - 15 min.

In the meantime, place the beet into a food processor and blend till it either has smooth paste consistency or is finely chopped. Spread onto the baked dough and distribute all the other toppings as desired.

For salad, chop all the ingredients into small size and place them in a bowl. Garnish with thyme.

One small pizza this size is plenty for a parrot.

HEALTHY VEGGIE TRUFFLES

INGREDIENTS

1/4 cup cauliflower, diced, steamed

1/4 cup green squash, diced, steamed

1/4 cup sweet potato, steamed

1 tbsp yellow split peas, cooked

1 tbsp almond flour or almond flakes

2 tbsp rolled barley

2 tbsp flax seeds

2 tbsp coconut flour

2 tbsp quinoa, cooked or sprouted

Soaked almonds (quantity depends
    on number of truffles)

INSTRUCTIONS

Cut the cauliflower, green squash, and sweet potato into small cubes, place them into a steamer basket, and cover. Remove when tender and let cool. Cook the yellow peas. Mash everything with a fork, then add cooked yellow peas, tablespoon of almond flour, and mix it well. Form small truffles size of 3 cm / 1 inch in diameter. Hide a whole almond in each truffle, then roll and coat them individually in rolled barley, flax seeds, coconut flour, and cooked quinoa.

Place each into a different color paper baking cup to create a colorful variety platter for your bird to explore. Mine just loved tearing apart those strange looking paper baking cups.

...SIDE SALAD

INGREDIENTS

Beet

Kell

Brussels sprouts

INSTRUCTIONS

For salad, chop kell and brussels sprouts, and add raw beet shavings.

ROASTED BUTTERNUT SQUASH, OKRA SKEWERS WITH SWEET POTATO CHIPS

INGREDIENTS

4 butternut squash cubes

2-3 okra pieces

1 tsp dry oregano

1/2 cup sweet potato

1 scotch bonnet chili pepper, to garnish

1 tbsp raw coconut oil

INSTRUCTIONS

Preheat the oven to 177 °C /350 °F

Cut the butternut squash into large cubes and sweet potato into chunky chips then drizzle with melted coconut oil. Sprinkle butternut squash cubes with oregano. Place onto parchment paper on a baking tray and bake for about 40 minutes or until tender. Make sure it doesn't burn.

Take it out of the oven and leave to cool. In the meantime, slice the okra onto thick rounds. Thread roasted butternut squash and okra onto bamboo skewers.

TIP: *This can be served individually.*

FENNEL DILL SALAD

INGREDIENTS

1/2 raw fennel, finely sliced

1 tbsp dry organic rose hips (optional)

1 sprig of dill, finely chopped

2 baby sweetcorn

Handful of watercress (optional)

Soaked

1 tbsp milk thistle seeds

1 tbsp amaranth grain

INSTRUCTIONS

Finely slice fennel and baby sweetcorn, then add chopped dill, a spoonful of dry rose hips, soaked milk thistle, and amaranth seeds. Toss gently and serve in a favorite bowl.

PARROT'S VEGETABLE STIR FRY

INGREDIENTS

2 tbsp pearl barley, cooked

2 tbsp raw broccoli, finely chopped

1/2 carrot, cut into strips

1/4 cup pak choi, (bok choy), chopped

1/4 cup yellow bell pepper, cut into thin strips

5 sugar snap peas, chopped

5 green beans

2 brussels sprouts, cut into thin strips

1 tbsp raw coconut oil

2 cashews (crushed)

1 chili pepper

Soaked

1 tbsp sesame seeds

INSTRUCTIONS

Chop up all the vegetables and gently stir fry in coconut oil until al dente on very low heat. Don't overcook. Meanwhile, combine barley and water in a pot and bring to a boil. Reduce heat, cover, and simmer until tender.

Put cooked barley in a bowl and place the vegetables on top. Sprinkle with crushed cashews, sesame seeds, and chopped chili pepper and let it cool.

This can be served also over brown rice, sprouted or cooked quinoa, or raw courgette.

PARROT'S RAW "COLESLAW"

INGREDIENTS

1/4 cup cauliflower, roughly chopped

1 carrot, shredded

2 tbsp white cabbage, shredded

1/4 cup pak choi (bok choy), thinly chopped

Sprouted

2 tbsp mung beans

2 tbsp rye groats

Soaked

2-3 tbsp raw cashews

1 tbsp water

INSTRUCTIONS

Chop the cauliflower and mix it with shredded carrot and cabbage, add thinly sliced pak choi.

Place the soaked cashews in a blender with a tablespoon of water, and blend till you get a thick paste. Add more water if required to create a "creamy" paste. Transfer all the chopped vegetables into a bowl and add the cashew paste then toss gently to combine. Sprinkle with sprouted mung beans and rye groats.

VEGETABLE "SUSHI " ROLL

INGREDIENTS

1/2 cup brown rice, cooked

1/4 cup sweet potato, steamed

1/2 cup raw broccoli, finely chopped

Radish, green peas, green bell pepper, and cucumber, to garnish

Pansy flowers (optional)

INSTRUCTIONS

Put brown rice and water together in a pot. Bring the rice/water to a boil, uncovered, and cook till tender. Place the diced sweet potato into a steamer basket and cover. Steam until tender. Finely chop broccoli and mix it with mashed sweet potato and rice. Form small balls about 3cm/1 inch in diameter.

Place them onto bamboo plate and decorate with small pieces of radish, cucumber, green peas, slices of bell pepper. Flowers will always make it more attractive.

Your bird will enjoy not only shredding the food but also the "plate."

VEGETABLES PICK A MIX

INGREDIENTS

1/2 carrot

1/4 cucumber

1/4 courgette (zucchini)

2 tbsp butternut squash

1/2 yellow bell pepper

2 tbsp raw sweetcorn

INSTRUCTIONS

Chop all the vegetables into small cubes and mix with all other ingredients. Add about 1 tablespoon of veggie mix into a colorful paper baking cup. If using mini baking cups place 1 teaspoon of the veggie mix.

Your feathered companion will have toy and food all in one.

Sprouted

1 tbsp buckwheat

1 tbsp mung beans

1 tbsp oats (unhulled)

Soaked

1 tbsp almonds

1 tbsp sunflower seeds

PAK CHOI PARCELS

INGREDIENTS

3 outer pak choi (bok choy) leaves,
   lightly steamed

1/4 cup raw green squash,
   finely chopped

1 tsp brown rice, cooked

Sprouted

1 tbsp kamut

1 tbsp amaranth

1 tbsp barley (unhulled)

1 tbsp chickpeas (garbanzo beans)

1 tbsp alfalfa

INSTRUCTIONS

To assemble the parcels, steam the pak choi
leaves for about 2 minutes until softened.

In a separate bowl mix the diced raw squash
with cooked rice and sprouts.

Place the leaf on a board and put a spoonful of
the filling in the center of the leaf, then roll the
stem-end over the filling, fold in the sides and
carefully roll up the parcels so the filling
remains enclosed.

Serve on parrot-safe bamboo or edible plate
with any extra toppings on the side.

TRADITIONAL BRITISH OPEN SANDWICH

INGREDIENTS

2 tbsp split green peas, cooked

1 tsp raw sweetcorn

2 slices of red bell pepper

3 slices of cucumber

Salad watercress microgreens, to garnish

1 tsp flax seeds

Sprouted

1 tbsp fenugreek seeds

1 tbsp barley (unhulled)

1 tbsp clover seeds

1 tbsp brown rice

1 tbsp chickpeas (garbanzo beans)

BREAD

Make the bread first. For bread recipe please go to chapter Snacks, Breads, and Treats and use Zen's seed loaf recipe.

INSTRUCTIONS

Cook the green peas, drain, and blend using a food processor. Once blended, mix in the flax seeds.

Cut a slice of the bread about 1 cm thick (1/4 inch) and spread a thin layer of the mashed-up peas then add the remaining toppings.

Vegetable - Fruit soups

Soups for parrots may be a bit unusual but can still be refreshing and full of nutrients. Soup is easily digestible and its creamy texture can be interesting to them. This is another way of getting some nutrients to our feathered friends.

Tip: All raw soups should be served at room temperature. Do not re-heat. Can be refrigerated up to one day.

Safety Tip: Always remove any pits and seeds. Some serving dishes were used for photo purposes only and are not recommended for your bird. Always use bird-safe dishes.

BEET - CAULIFLOWER SOUP - RAW

INGREDIENTS

1 raw beet

1/2 cup cauliflower, chopped

1/4 cup raw coconut water
   or cold filtered water

1 tbsp curly parsley, finely chopped

1 tbsp almonds, roughly chopped,
   to garnish

Pansy edible flowers, to garnish

INSTRUCTIONS

Place all the ingredients including coconut
water into your food processor and blend until
nice and smooth. Add more coconut water
if consistency is too thick.

Garnish with roughly chopped almonds,
parsley, and edible flowers.

PEPPER - CUCUMBER SOUP - RAW

INGREDIENTS

1 red bell pepper

1 cup cucumber, peeled and diced

1/4 cup water (adjust to desired consistency)

2 tbsp fresh parsley

2 tbsp fresh dill, to garnish

1 tsp flax seeds, to garnish

1 tbsp pecan nuts, chopped

INSTRUCTIONS

Place all the ingredients into your food
processor and blend until nice and smooth.
Add more water if consistency is too thick.

Serve chilled. Garnish with a sprig of fresh dill,
sprinkle with flax seeds and pecans.

PARROT'S GARDEN SOUP - RAW

INGREDIENTS

1 yellow bell pepper

4 radishes

1/2 courgette (zucchini), chopped

1/2 cup kale

1/4 cup parsley

1/4 cup coriander (cilantro)

1 cup water (adjust to desired consistency)

1 tbsp cashews, to garnish

1 tbsp hemp seeds, to garnish

INSTRUCTIONS

Place all the ingredients into your food processor and blend until nice and smooth. Garnish with any combination of chopped vegetables and sprinkle with hemp seeds and cashews.

BROCCOLI - PAK CHOI SOUP - COOKED

INGREDIENTS

1/2 pak choi (bok choy)

1/4 cup broccoli, chopped

1 slice of swede

1/2 carrot

1 tsp raw coconut oil

1 tsp fresh mint, chopped

1/4 cup water

1 walnut, to garnish

1 scotch bonnet chilli pepper, to garnish

INSTRUCTIONS

Heat the raw coconut oil in a pan on very low heat until it has just melted. Sauté all finely chopped vegetables for about 5 minutes, except the mint. Stir continuously so it won't burn. Add water and bring to a lively simmer over medium heat and cook until tender.

Remove from heat and transfer the soup to a blender and puree until smooth. Thin with boiled water if soup is too thick. Pour into a bowl and garnish with walnut and chopped chili peppers and let it cool.

Serve mildly warm. May refrigerate up to 3 days.

Safety Tip: Coconut oil has a smoking point 177 degrees Celcius. (350 °F) No oil should be heated above its smoking point. It will melt at about 25 degrees C. (77 °F)

Safety Tip:
Never serve your bird anything hot.

BUTTERNUT SQUASH - CARROT SOUP - COOKED

INGREDIENTS

1 cup butternut squash, diced

1 carrot, peeled and chopped

1/4 cup sweet potato, diced

1 tsp of raw coconut oil

Pumpkin seeds, to garnish

1 sprig of parsley

INSTRUCTIONS

Heat the raw coconut oil in a pan on very low heat until it has just melted. Saute all finely chopped vegetables on very low heat for about 5 minutes, except pumpkin seeds. Stir continuously so it won't burn. Add water and bring to a lively simmer over medium heat and cook until tender. Remove from heat and transfer the soup to a blender and puree until smooth. Thin with boiled water if soup is too thick. Let it cool. Pour into a bowl and garnish with pumpkin seeds (pepitas) and chopped parsley.

Tip: *Serve at room temperature. May be refrigerated for up to 3 days.*

CHILI PEPPER WATERMELON SOUP - RAW

INGREDIENTS

1/4 cup watermelon, coarsely chopped

1/4 cup cucumber, chopped

1/4 of green bell pepper

1 chili pepper

1/4 red apple, skinless and diced

1 sprig of fresh curly parsley,
   to garnish

Tip: *This soup is more suitable during summer and can be quite refreshing for your bird.*

INSTRUCTIONS

Place all the ingredients except the apples into a food processor and blend until nice and smooth, and no large pieces remain.

Sprinkle with diced apples and finely chopped chili pepper. Finish it off with a sprig of curly parsley.

SNACKS, BREADS & TREATS

Treats are a great way to reward your bird during training or simply because they are so adorable.

What I was trying to achieve with these recipes was to share that it helps to know exactly what you are feeding your bird companion when you choose to reward them.

Homemade treats are the best you can offer your parrot as there are no artificial colorings, saturated fats, preservatives, or cheap fillers. Even if it is just a treat, you're still giving your bird a healthy reward.

REMEMBER THESE ARE TREATS
SO FEED SPARINGLY!

Ceylon Cinnamon VS Cassia Cinnamon

When including cinnamon in your bird's diet it is important to know which of these two is actually safe for your precious companion. **Ceylon Cinnamon** (sourced from the plant Cinnamomum Zeylanicum) is from Sri Lanka. Also called "true cinnamon," it has a sweeter, more delicate flavor than cassia does. **Cassia Cinnamon** comes from a different plant called Cinnamomum Cassia. But only Ceylon Cinnamon is safe for your bird and here are some reported facts.

True cinnamon, Ceylon, is packed with antioxidants and helps fight fungal infections, regulates blood sugar and has inflammatory properties.

However, the two varieties, Cassia and Ceylon, contain the same flavoring substance called Coumarin, a blood thinner that is toxic and can cause liver damage or complete failure. Cassia cinnamon contains 1000 times higher levels of coumarin than Ceylon, so consuming it over a prolonged period of time can have serious consequences. Imagine a tiny birds' system.

So how do you tell the difference between Ceylon and Cassia Cinnamon? Here is a guide to buy the right cinnamon. If you are buying powdered, make sure the label says **Ceylon Cinnamon**.

Ceylon Cinnamon	Cassia/Chinese Cinnamon
Expensive	Commonly available and cheap
Tan brown in color	Reddish dark brown color
Thin and paper-like textured bark that forms multiple layers when rolled	Uneven thick bark that forms only a few layers when rolled
Fragile, easily broken	Tough, difficult (if not impossible) to grind into powder with an electric home kitchen grinder
Delicate, sweet with subtle notes of clove	Strong taste

APPLE, BLUEBERRY & MANGO BOWL WITH COMPOTE

INGREDIENTS

1/2 red apple, skinless & seedless

1 tbsp mango, chopped

1 tbsp blueberries

1 tbsp pomegranate seeds

1 tsp chia seeds

1 tsp Ceylon cinnamon

Compote

1/4 cup blackberries

1/4 cup blueberries

Soaked

1 tbsp pecan nuts, chopped

INSTRUCTIONS

Chop the apples and mango into small cubes, and place in your birds' favorite bowl. Sprinkle with cinnamon and add some whole blueberries.

For the compote, place the blackberries and blueberries in a medium saucepan with ¼ cup water. Bring to a boil then reduce to a simmer and cover. Simmer 10-15 minutes until fruit is tender. Mash with fork to desired consistency.

Pour the compote over the chopped fruit and sprinkle with chia seeds, roughly chopped pecan nuts (can be whole), and pomegranate seeds.

FORAGING TREAT

INGREDIENTS

Green pepper

Pak choi (Bok choy)

Butternut squash

Radish

Cucumber

Brussel sprouts

Beet

Swede

Sweet potato - lightly steamed or raw

INSTRUCTIONS

Thread the chunky pieces of vegetable onto a leather strip or a long stainless steel skewer that you can hang in the cage.

BUTTERNUT SQUASH CUPCAKES

INGREDIENTS

1 cup spelt flour

1 tbsp coconut and almond flour

1/2 cup to 1 cup home-made butternut squash, puree (not from a tin as that can contain additives or preservatives)

1 free range egg

1/4 cup raw cranberries, rinsed and chopped

1/2 cup wheat germ

2 tbsp flax seeds

1/2 cup of dry oats

1 tbsp millet

1/2 cup shredded carrots (use food processor)

1/2 cup water

2 tbsp almonds and pecan nuts, chopped

1/2 Ceylon cinnamon stick, crushed

2 tbsp raw coconut oil

Hulled sesame seeds, to garnish

INSTRUCTIONS

Preheat the oven to 177 °C /350 °F

To create your home-made butternut squash puree, steam the butternut squash and once soft, blend it in the food processor to a smooth paste. Then combine all the ingrediencies in a medium sized bowl and mix well.

Half fill mini paper baking cups with the mix and sprinkle with sesame seeds, then bake until golden brown (about 30 minutes, oven depending). Ensure it is cooked all the way through.

ALTERNATIVE

Filling the batter into a walnut shell will create great foraging treat for your bird. Simply split the walnut shell in half, take out the nut and fill in the batter and bake it.

ZEN'S SEED LOAF

INGREDIENTS

2 ripe bananas, mashed

2-3 carrots, cooked & blended

2 organic strawberries, blended

1 cup rolled oats

1 tbsp black quinoa

2 tbsp flax seeds

3 tbsp pumpkin seeds

2 tbsp sesame seeds

2 tbsp chia seeds

2-4 tbsp milk thistle seeds

1/2 cup almonds, chopped roughly

1 tbsp walnuts, crushed

1 tbsp hazelnuts, crushed

2 tablespoons raw coconut oil

1 cup of water

Tip: *Whether you wish to make one serving or a large batch, you can always adjust the quantities of the ingredients as desired. It can be frozen in single batches and defrosted when required.*

Cooking Tip: *Flax or chia seeds with a little water added to them will form a very nice and healthy egg substitute for bread.*

Safety Tip: *Always ensure all baked treats are cooled down before offered to your bird.*

INSTRUCTIONS

Preheat the oven to 177 °C /350 °F .
First peel and cut the carrots into small chunks and place them into a pot of boiling water. (Can also be steamed). Once cooked, let cool and using a food processor, blend the carrots and strawberries. In a separate bowl mix all the dry ingredients together. Add carrots and strawberry mix, and combine. Add water as required to create a soft batter, and two tablespoons of melted coconut oil.

Put the batter into a loaf pan that you grease with coconut oil. Or you may use any type of a large, deep cookie cutter that you can place on a flat baking tray with parchment paper underneath and fill it in with the batter. Be sure to grease your cookie-cutter sides also. Spread it evenly. Bake for 20-25 minutes

Once baked remove it from the oven, flip it over, and bake for another 30 minutes. Slice it once cooled.It can also be frozen.

VEGGIE BISCUITS

INGREDIENTS

1/4 of sweet potato, steamed

1 cup green squash, steamed

1 beet, steamed

1 carrot, steamed

1/2 banana

1 chili pepper

1 tbsp raw coconut flakes

1/2 cup almonds

1/4 cup millet

1 tbsp pumpkin seeds

INSTRUCTIONS

Preheat the oven to 177 °C /350 °F .

Cut the sweet potato, green squash, beet, and carrot into small pieces and place them into steamer basket and cover. Remove once tender and let cool. Use dinner fork to thoroughly mash all steamed vegetables and place them into a medium sized bowl. Mix in mashed banana, finely chopped chili pepper, coconut flakes, almonds, millet, pumpkin seeds, and mix it well. From the dough, form small balls then squash them. Create round biscuit shapes.

Bake for 20 -25 minutes. Once baked, remove from the oven, flip it over, and bake for another 30 minutes. Sprinkle with coconut flour.

JOLLY GRAIN BAKE

INGREDIENTS

1 red apple, seedless and peeled

2 tbsp raw or dried cranberries

2 tbsp flax seeds

1 tbsp dried rose hips

1 tbsp amaranth

2 tbsp buckwheat

2 tbsp milk thistle seeds

1 Ceylon cinnamon stick

2 tbsp dried, frozen, or fresh blueberries

2 tbsp hulled sesame seeds

2 tbsp oat groats

3 tbsp barley flakes

2 tbsp brown rice

2 tbsp coconut flakes

Water

INSTRUCTIONS

Mix all the ingredients in a bowl and transfer onto the baking tray or glass oven-safe dish. Sprinkle with crushed cinnamon stick.

Pour water over it to cover the whole mix (approx. 1cm above the mix), stir well to distribute water evenly. Cover with foil or lid, and bake at 177 °C /350 °F for about an hour until the water is absorbed.

Check midway through baking to be sure mix is not burning. Add more water if needed. Remove from oven when it is done and let it cool.

Portion it after cooling and store it in Ziploc® bags for freezing.

VEGETABLE GRAIN BAKE

INGREDIENTS

4 tbsp mung beans

4 tbsp black quinoa

1 tbsp wild rice

1 tbsp barley

1 tbsp buckwheat

2 tbsp amaranth grain

1 tbsp chickpeas (garbanzo beans)

1 carrot, sliced

1 tbsp raw sweetcorn

2 tbsp split peas, yellow or green

1/2 cup raw broccoli florets, chopped

1 tbsp flax seeds

1 chili pepper

2 sprigs fresh thyme

INSTRUCTIONS

Mix all the ingredients in a bowl and transfer onto the baking tray or glass oven-safe dish.

Pour water over it to cover the whole mix (approx. 1cm above the mix), stir well to evenly distribute water. Cover with foil or lid and bake at 177 °C /350 °F for about an hour until the water is absorbed.

Check midway through baking to be sure mix is not burning. Add more water if needed. Remove from oven when it is done and let it cool.

Portion it after cooling and store it in Ziploc® bags for freezing.

QUICK FIX TREAT

INGREDIENTS

1/4 ripe yellow plantains
    (if not ripe then can be gently
    fried in raw coconut oil on very
    low heat or cooked)

1 tsp chia seeds

Dry rosehips, almonds, cashews to garnish

INSTRUCTIONS

Cut the plantains into about 2cm (1/2 inch) thick rounds. Place it on a plate or in their favorite bowl and sprinkle with chia seeds then garnish with rosehips and nuts.

Tip: *If you are in hurry or simply have no time to spend in the kitchen baking, this is a quick way to treat your feathered friend. You can always substitute for fresh banana.*

INSTRUCTIONS

Preheat the oven to 177 °C /350 °F

Combine flax seeds and sesame seeds in a bowl and set aside. Place the figs, carrot, cooked swede, broccoli, chili pepper, and parsley into a food processor. Put mixture in a separate bowl and combine with 1 tablespoon of coconut oil and grated raw coconut. Place the pistachios, almonds, and sunflower seeds in a food processor and process to a crumbly texture. Add the nut mixture to the vegetable mixture, together with cumin seeds. Mix it well.

Form the mixture into balls 3-4 cm (1 1/4 - 1 1/3 inch) diameter. Roll the balls in the flax/sesame mix to coat well. Place on a baking tray with parchment paper and bake for about 20-25 minutes, until crisp on the outside but still soft inside.

FALAFEL TREATS

INGREDIENTS

2 tbsp flax seeds

2 tbsp sesame seeds

3 raw figs (do not use dried figs)

1/4 cup swede, chopped and cooked

1/4 cup broccoli, chopped

1 carrot

1 tbsp almonds

1 tbsp pistachios

1 tsp cumin seeds

1 tbsp parsley, finely chopped

1 tbsp chili pepper, finely chopped

1 tbsp raw coconut, grated

1 tbsp raw coconut oil

Soaked

1 tbsp sunflower seeds

NUTTY COOKIES

INGREDIENTS

1/2 cup barley flour

1/4 cup teff

2 tbsp millet

1 cup rolled oats

3/4 cup walnuts, coarsely chopped

1 cup almonds, coarsely chopped

8 tbsp raw coconut oil, melted and cooled

1 egg

1 tsp Ceylon cinnamon powder

Water as required

INSTRUCTIONS

Preheat the oven to 177 °C /350 °F .

Pour contents into medium sized bowl. Stir in melted, cooled coconut oil, egg, and teaspoon of Ceylon cinnamon. Add water if the dough is too dry. Roll the dough into tablespoon-sized balls, place onto a parchment-lined tray and flatten with your fingers. Sprinkle with chia seeds, and bake until edges are set for about 15-20 minutes.

SMOOTHIES

Smoothies are easy to make, endlessly versatile, and you can deliver the nutritious goods while not worrying that your flock will turn up their beaks at something green. You can add seeds to boost the nutrition or add extra ingredients. It's a great way to introduce healthy greens to a fussy parrot. See Chapter **Pure Water** for more advice on what water is the best for your bird.

HOW TO MAKE A PARROT SMOOTHIE

To make any of these smoothies simply place all the ingredients (except nuts) into a blender and blend until smooth. Add water if the consistency is too thick, and add chopped nuts or seeds. Use organic vegetables and fruit. Always wash the vegetables and fruit thoroughly and peel the skin off where required, as some skin can still contain pesticide residue. You can always adjust ingredients, quantities as required. Smoothies can be refrigerated for up to 1 day.

ZEN'S ULTIMATE SMOOTHIE

INGREDIENTS

1/2 pak choi (bok choy)

1 tbsp papaya, chopped

1 slice of mango

1 tbsp spinach

Raw, organic coconut water as needed

1 tbsp flax seeds

1 tsp of raw coconut oil

Safety Tip: Avoid commercially produced coconut water that may be processed and contains sugar, preservatives, or other components that could harm your bird. Always read the labels. You can always buy a whole, raw coconut, crack it and drain the water out.

FRESH ME UP

INGREDIENTS

1/2 cucumber

1/4 courgette (zucchini)

1 kiwi, peeled

Water as needed

1 tsp chia seeds

1 sprig of mint

HAPPY PARROT

INGREDIENTS

1 pear, cored

1 red apple, skinless & seedless

1 handful of broccoli

1 tbsp almonds,
    roughly chopped

1 sprig of mint

Water as needed

LET'S GET IT ON

INGREDIENTS

1 beet

1 carrot

1 handful of kale

1 sprig of fresh parsley

2 walnuts, roughly chopped

Safety Tip: Don't forget to remove pits from
all fruit as these are very toxic to parrots.

Health Tip: Use spinach in moderation as it is high in oxalates
which binds to calcium and makes it unavailable for absorption.

Nutritional Tip: Fruit sugars are great for birds as
long as it's part of a varied diet.

CLEAN AND GREEN

INGREDIENTS

1 handful of watercress

1 red apple, skinless, seedless

1 handful of kale

1 tbsp chia seeds

CJ LOVE

INGREDIENTS

1 banana

1 tbsp Brazil nuts, roughly chopped

4 organic strawberries

1 tbsp blueberries

1 sprig of mint

SUMMER SMOOTHIE

INGREDIENTS

1 slice of watermelon

4 organic strawberries

1 tbsp grated raw coconut

1 tsp chia seeds

Tip:
Watermelon seeds are safe for parrots

WARNING! *Avoid using glasses as a serving dish to your birds. Drinks were photographed in clear glasses, so the color and consistency can be seen better.*

FRUIT SORBET

It's simple, fun, and raw! This will not only keep your bird occupied but it's a great treat to cool them down in very hot weather. You can experiment by trying to combine different types of fruits and vegetables.

SAFETY TIP: Remember always wash fruits and vegetables before using.

Lolly sticks (or popsicle sticks) aren't necessary, but are nice to include as they will help your bird to hold them firmly while munching. Use only safe wooden sticks that are designed for contact with the food. To make larger batches you can always adjust the ingredient quantities.

MANGO LOLLY

INSTRUCTIONS

INGREDIENTS

1 cup mango, diced

2 organic strawberries

1 sprig of mint

Raw coconut water

1 wooden stick

Place mango, strawberries, and mint in a blender or food processor and blend on high speed till smooth. Add the coconut water as needed.

Pour the mixture into ice lolly molds, then pop a stick into each one. You can place a small mint leaf into the bottom of the mold.
Freeze it for a few hours.

PAPAYA - KIWI LOLLY

INGREDIENTS

1 cup papaya, diced and seedless

1 kiwi

1 tsp chia seeds

INSTRUCTIONS

Peel the papaya and remove any seeds, cut both kiwi & papaya into larger pieces. Place them into a blender or food processor and blend on high speed till smooth. Stir in chia seeds.

Pour the mixture into ice lolly molds, then pop a stick into each one.

Freeze it for a few hours.

APPLE - PEAR CRUMBLE

INGREDIENTS

1/2 red apple, peeled, chopped

1/2 pear, peeled, chopped

3 pecan nuts, roughly chopped

INSTRUCTIONS

Combine the fruit ingredients and place them in a blender or food processor and blend on high speed till smooth.
Stir in crushed pecans.

Pour the mixture into ice lolly molds, then pop a stick into each one. Freeze it for a few hours.

Saftey Tip: Avoid using Granny Smith apples as they are too acidic for parrots.

RAW MANGO COCONUT BALLS

INGREDIENTS

1/2 fresh mango

1/4 cup organic raspberries

1/4 raw coconut, diced

1 tsp almond flour

1 tbsp raw coconut oil

2 tbsp coconut flour

INSTRUCTIONS

Place the mango, raspberries, and raw coconut into a food processor and blend until smooth; then add 1 tbsp of coconut oil and mix it for another minute. Add teaspoon of almond flour. If consistency is too liquidy add more almond flour.

Form the mixture into small balls and roll them in coconut flour. Place onto a tray and put it into the freezer for half hour.

TUTTI FRUITY MIX

INGREDIENTS

Apple

Strawberries

Grape

Banana

Mint leaf

Water

INSTRUCTIONS

Cut all the ingredients into small pieces and place into a suitable mold or plastic cup. Pour in water so it only covers the fruit and place long wooden stick in the middle.

Leave in freezer for at least 5 hours and serve it in a feeding bowl or on a plate and let the fun begin.

BLUEBERRIES CRUMBLE

INGREDIENTS

2 tbsp raw blueberries, whole

2 tbsp raw blueberries, crushed

2 tbsp hazelnuts, crushed

INSTRUCTIONS

Place the nuts into a food processor and blend till finely crushed. For this lolly I have used small plastic cups. Place the nut crumble at the bottom of the cup and cover with whole blueberries then add another thick layer of blended blueberries. Freeze it for few hours. Pop lolly out of plastic cup and serve.

FOREST MIX

INGREDIENTS

1/4 cup organic raspberries, whole

1/4 cup organic strawberries,
  roughly chopped

1/4 cup blueberries, whole

1 tbsp almonds, whole or chopped

1 tbsp cashews

*You can substitute raw coconut
water for regular water*

INSTRUCTIONS

Combine all the ingredients, add raw coconut water, and place a spoonful into a small plastic cup or larger lolly molds. Leave it in a freezer for at least 5 hours. Serve it in a feeding bowl or on a plate and let the fun begin during the hot summer days.

KARMEN BUDAI

Karmen is originally from a small country in Europe called Slovakia, a popular holiday destination for tourists visiting the country's beautiful mountains. Since childhood, she had a creative streak, which led to studying fashion design in her college years. Fashion remained a hobby and she moved on to a career in the corporate environment. She moved to the United Kingdom in 2004, intending only to stay for a few years, but settled there with her family. She has a beautiful son, and the most demanding, feathered, velcro cockatoo, called Polly, that consumes a majority of the family time. Polly is a toddler that will never grow up.

There are also new additions to the family of five delightful budgies.

Karmen's passion to contribute to the limited knowledge available on healthy food for parrots led to the creation of this book and its wide variety of nutritious recipes.

SHEAN PAO

Shean grew up along the West Coast. As a girl, she began writing poetry and short stories. She became a published author in 2016 when her book was chosen by NYT best-selling author, David Farland, to be the first in his David Farland Discovery Program.

Shean has been devoted to birds all her life, owning numerous parrots and rescuing wild birds. She joined Parrot Station in 2017, became Marlene's lead administrator, and helped grow Parrot Station from 3,000 members to over 56,000 in under a year.

Shean is also a graphic designer and runs an award-winning design and photography business with her husband. They reside in California with three marvellous talking creatures—Zen and Anaiah, African Grey Parrots, and CJ, a Sun Conure.

DR. JASON CREAN

Jason J. Crean, MS Bio, EdD is a degreed biologist, an avid aviculturist specializing in the propagation of softbill species, President of The Avicultural Society of Chicagoland, and First Vice-President and Education Chair for the American Federation of Aviculture.

Dr. Crean often speaks to avicultural groups across the country and acts as consultant to zoos and other institutions, including the Wildlife Genetics lab at Loyola Medical Center and Chicago's Nature Museum. He also runs a live animal education program that does free interactive programs for a host of different audiences.

Dr. Crean is also a biology instructor and has acted as a consulting curriculum designer and instructor in the Education Department at the Chicago Zoological Society.

Dr. Crean teaches courses in the Department of Biology at Saint Xavier University-Chicago including Zoo Biology: Animal Nutrition, Behavior, and Husbandry as well as Vertebrate Zoology and others.

Dr. Crean has been awarded the Presidential Award for Excellence in Science Teaching, the highest award an educator can receive in the US, by President Obama in 2009, the 2010 High School Science Teacher of the Year by the American Association for the Advancement of Science, as well as awards from the National Science Teachers Association, the National Association of Biology Teachers, the Illinois Science Teachers Association, the Golden Apple Foundation, among others.

He serves as President for the Illinois Science Teachers Association, President for the Illinois Association of Biology Teachers, and sits on the Board of Directors for the Association of Presidential Awardees in Science Teaching and the College Board's National Science Advisory Panel.

Dr. Crean also runs Avian Raw Whole Food Nutrition on Facebook.

DR. STEPHANIE LAMB

Stephanie Lamb, DVM, Dipl ABVP, has always desired to provide good health, happiness, and care to all animals. She grew up in Las Vegas, NV and after graduating from UNLV with a B.S. in Biology, she attended veterinary school at the University of Minnesota. Upon finishing veterinary school she performed a one-year internship in avian and exotic medicine followed by a two-year residency in avian medicine and surgery in Wilton, CT. After completing her residency, Dr. Lamb worked in southern California and Arizona at exotics-exclusive animal hospitals. During this time she gained extensive knowledge and became skilled in treating exotic mammals, birds, reptiles, amphibians, and wildlife. During her career she has also worked with many humane societies, parrot, and rabbit rescue groups, wildlife centers and raptor rehabilitation facilities. She is always striving to learn more and is focused on contributing to the advancement of knowledge of avian and exotic animal medicine by providing the highest quality veterinary care possible.

She and her husband share their home with dogs, geckos, fish, and 13 birds. Dr. Lamb passed her Avian Medicine boards in the fall of 2014. She has publications in peer reviewed journals about avian and exotic mammal medicine and has lectured at county, state, and national veterinary conferences about avian medicine. She has also spoken to local bird, reptile, and rabbit clubs in her community.

MARLENE MC'COHEN

Marlene Mc'Cohen was born in Oldham, England. She is an actress and producer, known for It's Always Sunny in Philadelphia (2005), Interstellar Wars (2016) and Captain Battle: Legacy War (2013). She is also the producer of the fun short, Sniffers (2017) for her bird fans.

Marlene has been an avid parrot lover from a young age with extensive experience and research into the care and training of parrots. Her goal is to educate parrot owners and enhance the life of parrot companions world-wide using social media. She currently has over 95,000 YouTube followers and over 64,000 members on her Facebook group, Parrot Station.

Marlene uses stories to educate her followers and show them what it is truly like to live with parrots. Marlene currently lives with six parrots, and it is clear from her videos that she is truly a parrot whisperer.

Sources

Avian Raw Whole Food Nutrition (Facebook Group)

This is aviculturist and biologist Jason Crean's private group that deals exclusively with raw, whole food nutrition in the feeding of birds. The philosophy of the group is simple: feeding an abundance of raw, whole foods is what our birds need to thrive.
www.beaksbirdhouse.com/nutrition

Dr. Jason Crean
Team THRIVE! Program

Join membership exclusive closed Facebook group

www.beaksbirdhouse.com/thrive

Stephanie Lamb, DVM Dipl ABVP

Arizona Exotic
Animal Hospital
www.azeah.com

WORLD PARROT TRUST

An international leader in science-based, results-oriented, parrot conservation and welfare efforts since1989. www.parrots.org
Facebook:@WorldParrotTrust
Twitter: @ParrotTrust

Please join us at
www.parrotsfinecuisine.com
to receive updates, giveaways and notifications of new books

If you would like to know more about advertising in *A Parrot's Fine Cuisine and Nutritional Guide*, please contact us at parrotsfinecuisine@hotmail.com.

Parrot Station (Facebook Group)

Created by: Marlene Mc'Cohen
This is a friendly group for all parrot lovers to communicate, educate, share parrot stories and introduce their parrots.

www.parrotstation.com
@marlenemccohen
#Engaged, Not Caged

Polly's Natural Parrot Boutique

www.pollysnaturalparrotboutique.com
info@pollysnaturalparrotboutique.com

Made in the USA
Monee, IL
03 May 2021